D1538883

THE
QUEST
OF
SETH

ESTHER CASIER QUINN

THE QUEST OF SETH

FOR THE OIL OF LIFE

THE UNIVERSITY OF CHICAGO PRESS

Library of Congress Catalog Card Number: 62-18120

THE UNIVERSITY OF CHICAGO PRESS, CHICAGO & LONDON
The University of Toronto Press, Toronto 5, Canada

© *1962 by The University of Chicago. All rights reserved*
Published 1962. Composed and printed by
THE UNIVERSITY OF CHICAGO PRESS,
Chicago, Illinois, U.S.A.

To Vincent

who shared the Quest

PREFACE

THIS STUDY was begun in 1949 at the suggestion of Professor Roger Sherman Loomis of Columbia University. As he pointed out, there appear in certain Middle English works—notably Mandeville's *Travels,* Caxton's translation of the *Legenda Aurea,* and Malory's *Morte Darthur*—legends, which, although not identical, resemble each other sufficiently to be considered part of a single complex; these legends concern Seth, Solomon, and the wood of the cross.

Preliminary investigation proved the field far vaster than had been anticipated; there were many other versions in English, as well as versions in Latin and in most other European languages. There was, moreover, virtually no modern scholarship on the subject; many areas were almost completely unexplored. The immediate problem was to narrow the field of study. It seemed that before sound relationships among these versions could be established, the origin should be determined. I have, therefore, chosen to explore the beginnings of the legend and its early evolution.

This work is essentially an inquiry; its form has been largely determined by the material which has been uncovered. It was started with no preconceived hypothesis and has, apart from the obvious recognition that further work is necessary, arrived at only tentative conclusions. It would seem on the basis of the evidence assembled here that, although for its structure the legend was chiefly dependent on Christian theological concepts, the symbols and story-patterns may be traced to periods considerably antedating the Christian era.

The course of investigation has led to distant times, strange places, and unknown languages. These ramifications of the original subject have created problems, which I have attempted to solve with the materials at hand. Relative unfamiliarity with many of these areas has made impossible anything but a preliminary survey.

There has been no previous study of this sort. I am, however, indebted for particular aspects of the inquiry to a number of scholars whose works are mentioned in the text, footnotes, and bibliography. My warmest thanks are due to Professor Loomis, with whom this work was begun. To Professor W. T. H. Jackson I am most grateful for his careful reading of the manuscript, his many suggestions, and his continued encouragement. I wish also to thank Professor Elliot V. K. Dobbie and Professor A. Kent Hieatt for their kindness and scholarly counsel. Thanks are also due to Professor Howard Schless and Professor Moses Hadas. The comments of Professor Hadas on the first chapter in its early stages contributed materially, not only to the improvement of that chapter, but to the entire work. I wish finally to express my gratitude to the staffs of the three great libraries of Morningside Heights—those of Columbia University, the Union Theological Seminary, and the Jewish Theological Seminary. The present study would have been impossible without access to these superb collections.

The illustrations are taken from *The Legendary History of the Cross: A Series of Sixty-four Woodcuts from a Dutch Book Published by Veldener, A.D. 1483*, written and illustrated by John Ashton (London: T. Fisher Unwin, 1937).

CONTENTS

INTRODUCTION

DESPITE widespread current interest in myth, legend, and the hero, one of the most popular tales of the Middle Ages, the quest of Seth for the oil of mercy, remains almost totally unknown. Widely represented in the art and literature of nearly every European country over a period of hundreds of years, the legend has somehow escaped the attention of modern investigators. The existence of several Latin versions has not assured its inclusion in the expanding study of medieval Latin literature which has followed the work of Curtius.[1] Nor has the appearance of the legend in French, English, and German led to studies of the vernacular versions. Even its presence in medieval drama has failed to stimulate much investigation.

We shall explore presently the reasons for this neglect, but since the legend of Seth is generally so unfamiliar, we might first relate it briefly in one of its most typical forms. This version appears in the religious epic written in the North of England in the late thirteenth century, the *Cursor mundi*, one of the most popular and influential poems of the Middle Ages.[2] Within the larger drama of the *Cursor mundi*, which tells the story of the world from the Creation to the Judgment Day, our legend forms a kind of subplot: its episodes are not related as a unit but are interwoven throughout some 14,000 of the approximately 24,000 lines. The relevant parts may be summarized as follows:

When Adam is about to die, he bids his son Seth go to Paradise for the oil of mercy. The path will be apparent, since, as Adam and Eve left Paradise, their footprints were burned upon the grass, and no vegetation has ever grown there. Seth is refused the oil of mercy, but is granted three glimpses of Paradise. In the first he beholds a dry tree; in the second, an adder twined about the trunk; in the third, a newborn baby in the top. He is told that the dry tree and the serpent represent the sin of man and that the baby is Christ, who will be the oil of mercy. Seth receives three kernels of the tree of life and plants them in the mouth of his dead father. From the kernels three trees grow—a cedar, a cypress, and a pine—and remain growing in the vale of Hebron until the time of Moses.

These three trees are uprooted by Moses and become the wands with which he sweetens the waters of Marah and brings forth water from a rock.

David inherits the wands, which are now united to form a single staff. With it he changes the color and shape of some Ethiopians. The staff is replanted and grows into a tree.

Later Solomon attempts to use it in building his Temple, but in whatever way the tree is cut, it is always too long or too short. Perceiving its miraculous power, Solomon has the tree placed in the Temple.

One day a lady named Maximilla accidentally sits on the tree, and, when it bursts into flame, she is inspired to prophecy. The Jews, hearing that Christ will die upon this wood, put Maximilla to death and hurl the tree into a pit.

Miracles are performed until the tree is removed by the Jews and placed over a brook to serve as a bridge. The holy nature of the wood is announced by Sibyl, who refuses to walk on it and instead wades through the brook barefooted.

As the time of the Crucifixion approaches, a cross is made of the tree. The cross, however, cannot be lifted by any except Christ, since it was destined for him. By his dying on it he becomes the redeemer or the oil of mercy for mankind.[3]

These episodes are followed by the much better known sequel, the legend of the discovery of the cross.[4] The reasons for the greater familiarity of the story of Saint Helena and her search for the true cross are readily apparent. It is a clearly defined story, its versions resemble one another closely, and some of them are important works of literature—from Cynewulf's *Elene* in the eighth century[5] to Evelyn Waugh's *Helena* in the twentieth. The narrative is centered upon a single figure, an admirable and believable heroine, who has, moreover, some importance historically.

The essential difference between the Helena and Seth stories is this: the tale of Helena and her finding the cross belongs to the popular genre of the saint's legend; the tale of Seth and the cross is not really a legend at all; it is essentially a myth. Like most myths, it is etiological in character. It answered a question important to medieval men, especially after the discovery of the cross by Saint Helena: where had the wood come from which was used in the Crucifixion? To medieval man it was inconceivable that the great drama of redemption had been enacted on an ordinary tree; his mind was in readiness for—even in quest of—a story which would attribute to the wood a special origin and history prior to its ultimate destiny. The answer to the question, what was the origin of the tree, was pieced together over the centuries from a motley assortment of pre-existent materials. To trace the process of its formulation is the purpose of this study.

As for the hero, Seth, it is not difficult to perceive why he has remained unknown in modern times. He is unlike other medieval heroes, Lancelot and Tristram for instance, whose exploits in love and battle have endeared them to generations of readers. Seth is neither a warrior nor a lover; he has no conflicts, no passion. He is a simple, almost an abstract figure. Less fully developed as a man, he is a better archetype. Single-minded, he exists only to perform his mission, and it is a momentous one: he goes to fetch for mankind the gift of God's mercy. For suffering Adam is suffering mankind, and Seth seeks mercy not only for his father but for all men. Lacking passion and individuality, he is the perfect intermediary between sinful man and the divine creator; he is, in short, a type of Christ. Other Old Testament figures are considered types of Christ, but Seth, unlike them, had been given no part in the unfolding drama of the Old Testament; his role was completely apocryphal. He is, therefore, less well known, but not less interesting; less important historically, but more important mythologically. He is a new kind of medieval hero.

Despite the present unfamiliarity with the legend of Seth and the Holy Cross, it was enormously popular and widely dispersed in the Middle Ages, especially from the twelfth to the fifteenth centuries, appearing in dozens of versions not only in England, France, and Germany, but in Italy, Holland, Russia, Bulgaria, Iceland, and elsewhere, and, as late as the seventeenth century, making its appearance in Calderón's "Auto el Arbol del Mejor Fruto" and "La Sibila del Oriente y Gran Reina de Saba."[6] In England, though the legend was never transformed into great poetry, it was related in somewhat different versions in the following well-known books: the *Travels* of Sir John Mandeville,[7] Caxton's translation of the *Legenda Aurea*,[8]

The Quest of Seth

and Sir Thomas Malory's *Morte Darthur.*[9] There are allusions to it in a number of English mystery plays; it appears in the dramatic literature of France and Germany;[10] a complete version is dramatized in the Cornish *Origo mundi.*[11] In each of these works it forms, as in the *Cursor mundi*, a small part of a larger pattern. There are, however, a number of English texts devoted entirely to the narration of a fully developed Holy Cross legend: *The Holy Rode*, the *Story of the Holy Rood*, the *Canticum de Creatione*, and *The Holy Cross.*[12]

The legend of Seth and the Holy Cross was frequently represented not only in literature but also in art. It appeared at Troyes, in the windows of the churches of Saint Martin ès-Vignes, of Saint Pantaléon, of Sainte Madeleine, and of Saint Nizier.[13] It was frescoed on the walls of the choir of Santa Croce in Florence by Agnolo Gaddi.[14] Pietro della Francesca celebrated it in a series of frescoes in the chapel of the Bocci in the Church of San Francesco at Arezzo.[15] It was painted on the walls of the chapel of the Guild of the Holy Cross in the Church of the Trinity at Stratford-upon-Avon.[16] One of the most complete pictorial representations of the legend of Seth and the Holy Cross appears in the Dutch work, *Boec van den houte* (1483); here a series of sixty-four woodcuts depicts the legend from Seth's journey to Paradise to Helena's finding the Cross.[17]

Although the widespread appearance of the Seth legend in the literature and art of the Middle Ages has failed to arouse present-day interest, it did attract scholarly attention in the last century. An important pioneer study appeared in 1869—Adolfo Mussafia's "Sulla leggenda del legno della Croce."[18] Part of Arturo Graf's valuable book, *La leggenda del paradiso terrestre* (1878),[19] was devoted to the legend of the cross. The greatest contribution to a comprehensive study of the legend of Seth and the cross was made by Wilhelm Meyer in two important works, "*Vita Adae et Evae*" and "Die Geschichte des Kreuzholzes

vor Christus," the former appearing in 1879, the latter in
1882.[20] Meyer added considerably to the number of manuscripts which had been collected, provided a scheme for
the division of the legends into groups, and supplied a
very useful commentary. There are illuminating studies of
certain versions, especially Arthur S. Napier's Introduction
to his edition of the *History of the Holy Rood-Tree*[21] and
Albert Pauphilet's *Étude sur la queste del saint graal.*[22]

Short accounts of the legend have appeared from time
to time, but they have been mainly derived from Meyer.
Charles Mills Gayley in *Plays of Our Forefathers* (1907)[23]
deplored the current ignorance of the rood-tree legend
and attempted to reintroduce it. His account of the legend
—some twenty-five pages—is based almost entirely on
Meyer's and Napier's investigations. Another twenty-five-
page treatment of the rood-tree legends, in A. S. Rappoport's *Mediaeval Legends of Christ* (1935),[24] is also based
on Meyer.

Meyer's work is the nearest approach to a comprehensive study; yet it has certain limitations—apart from being
outdated and difficult to obtain: first, it is primarily a
textual study and is, therefore, very little concerned with
the origin of elements and the evolution and significance
of the legend; second, it has little to say of the English
versions. Indeed, Meyer's ignorance of the earliest extant
form of the rood-tree legend in the West—the version preserved in the Bodleian manuscript 343 and edited by
Napier—led him to certain erroneous conclusions. Meyer's
study suffers also, as Moses Gaster points out, from his
failure to consider early rood-tree legends in Slavonic.[25]
Neither Napier nor Pauphilet considers Meyer's study to
be entirely satisfactory. Pauphilet, for instance, wrote in
1921: "Malgré les travaux utiles et estimables de Mussafia,
A. Graf et W. Meyer, l'étude de la Légende de la Croix est
à refaire."[26]

To my knowledge, the kind of study recommended by

The Quest of Seth

Pauphilet has never been made. It is the basic assumption of *The Quest of Seth* that this legend, enormously popular in the Middle Ages but now unfamiliar to students and neglected by scholars, is a subject worthy of more attention than it has yet received.

Because of the dissemination of the legend throughout Europe over several centuries and because many areas are relatively uninvestigated, this cannot hope to be a definitive study, only a contribution toward such a study. We shall be especially concerned with the origins, the general pattern of evolution, and a typical fully developed version. It is hoped that the vastness and intricacy of the subject will in some measure excuse the inevitable gaps and errors and that, despite them, we may present with essential accuracy the main lines in the evolution of this legend.

The present work should be of particular interest to students concerned with the development of myth and legend, with the culture of the Middle Ages, and with the way in which pagan and Jewish traditions became interwoven in Christian thought.

For scholars interested in the formation of traditional stories this study will provide further data to illustrate the ways in which legends are shaped. Roger Sherman Loomis, in his study of the material used by Chrétien de Troyes, has compiled a list of the "ways of tradition."[27] As this study progresses it will be observed how frequently the legend of Seth and the Holy Cross developed in patterns similar to those which have been established for biblical, Homeric, and Arthurian stories.

As for the importance of understanding this legend if we are to appreciate the medieval achievement, we have only to note the number of versions which were created. Meyer alone lists over fifty. This widespread popularity of the legend throughout the Middle Ages establishes its importance in providing us with further insight into that complex phenomenon we call the medieval mind.[28]

Finally, the development of the Seth legend presents us

with another view of the Christian consciousness at work; it provides another example of the well-established pattern of discovering in alien material illustrations of Christian doctrine. Our legend will be found to belong to that enormous class of theologically motivated literature which has drawn upon the riches of the pagan and Jewish past and has, in the process, both preserved and changed old motifs and old stories.

The legend has been formed of elements from many sources. Certain episodes are derived from the Bible; others, from apocrypha and folklore. But despite the many episodes and the diverse sources from which these episodes stem, the legend has a kind of unity. It is primarily a theological rather than an artistic or dramatic unity: it is a unity based on the concept that as man's fall was occasioned by a tree, so man's redemption was achieved through a tree. So effective is the unifying power of this concept that it conceals the fact that the legend is not one, but two: first, the journey of Seth to Paradise and, second, the experiences of the wood which later became the cross.

In the pages which follow we shall trace in considerable detail the evolution of these two stories, separately and in their relation to each other. The process will be complicated, and it may be advisable to outline in advance the main stages in the development of the legend.

Investigation into the origin of the Seth legend reveals that the mission of Seth was not originally connected with the legend of the cross but considerably antedated Christianity. In the form in which it appears in the *Cursor mundi*, some elements are missing and others have been added, but the core is unmistakably an ancient Jewish apocryphal tale. Although of Jewish origin, the earliest extant version of the Seth legend is in Greek, the so-called *Apocalypse of Moses*, written in the first century A.D.[29] The form in which the legend of Seth passed into European literature is the Latin version of *The Apocalypse of Moses*, known as the *Vita Adae et Evae*.[30] Of particular interest at this early stage in the legend's development are the object of Seth's quest, "the oil of mercy," and the emergence of Seth as an apocryphal hero.

The first known instance of a Christian adoption of the Seth legend is the apocryphal *Gospel of Nicodemus*.[31] Originally composed in Greek, it was early translated into Latin and the vernacular. We read here that, at the time of the Harrowing of Hell, Seth told the patriarchs and prophets of his journey to Paradise; he then announced that Christ would bring the promised oil of mercy. This Christianization of the Seth legend was later inserted into the *Vita Adae et Evae*. As yet Seth was unconnected with the legend of the cross, but a crucial link had been established: Seth and his story had been absorbed into Christian legend. This interpolation from *The Gospel of Nicodemus* of the prophecy of Christ's coming was henceforth to be a constant element in the Seth story.

Meanwhile there appeared throughout Europe during the twelfth century a number of legends, some of them highly developed, recounting the origin of the wood from which the cross was made. Napier considers the earliest extant form of a rood-tree legend in the West to be an English version, preserved in the Bodleian manuscript 343. Here the history of the wood begins with Moses, who finds three rods; later, at the time of David, they grow together into a single trunk with three branches, each of a different kind—cedar, cypress, and pine. Solomon attempts to use the tree in the construction of the Temple, but however the wood is cut, it is always too long or too short. The tree is placed in the Temple, where a harlot prophesies the use of the wood in the Crucifixion. We have in the Bodleian version a number of key incidents which were to recur in many succeeding accounts. Most important are the tree with the three kinds of leaves and the prophesying harlot. The fact that there are close analogues in Old Slavonic introduces the subject of a possible Eastern origin of the rood-tree legends. Meyer considers the earliest version of

a rood-tree legend to be the Latin *Historia,* which he dates
before 1150.[32] Here the tree with the three kinds of leaves
first appears at the time of David. During Solomon's reign
it is the Queen of Sheba who prophesies that it will become the wood of the cross. These two traditions of
prophesying women—the harlot and the queen—were later
to be combined in the fully developed forms of the legend.

Representing the next step in the evolution of the rood-
tree legend is another group of stories; here the wood of
the cross is traced back to a tree in Paradise. The legend
at this stage falls into two main types; one in which the
cross originates in twigs and the other, in seeds brought
from Paradise. Of the twig type is the version in the
Pantheon of Geoffrey of Viterbo (*ca.* 1180).[33] Here a new
character appears—Hiontus—who we are told is a son of
Noah. This apocryphal son of Noah is carried to Paradise
and returns with three twigs—a fir, a palm, and a cypress.
These he plants in different places, but they come together
and grow into one tree. The rest of the story follows as in
the Bodleian version or in the *Historia,* except that the
prophesying Queen of Sheba appears as the Egyptian
queen, Nikaulé. The earliest known form of what we might
call the seed versions was interpolated into the *De imagine
mundi* of Honorius of Autun between 1154 and 1159.[34]
Although earlier than Geoffrey's version, it seems to belong to a later point in the evolution of the legend. A
number of innovations occur: most significant is the appearance of Adam in the story. It is related that he is
buried at Calvary, that an angel plants a kernel of the tree
of knowledge in his mouth, and that from this seed a
tree grows. This is the earliest version of the legend which
incorporates the concept that from the tree which caused
man's fall shall come man's redemption. The development
of this motif was influenced not only by doctrine, but also
by apocrypha and folklore. The other striking addition to
the legend is the fact that the already complex character,
the sibyl-queen of Sheba, has goosefeet! The explanation

The Quest of Seth

of how the Queen of Sheba got her goosefeet provides an illuminating example of the changes that occur when a story passes from one language and culture to another. The *De imagine mundi* version is also important as the earliest to state that the wood was used as a bridge. The *Pantheon* and the interpolation in the *De imagine mundi* represent two independent developments, which we might call the seed and the twig versions. It was the former pattern which was to prevail in most later versions.

The merging of the Seth and rood-tree legends seems to have occurred first with an interpolation into the *Vita Adae et Evae* of a Holy Cross legend.[35] The earliest extant version which relates the combined Seth and Holy Cross legends is Johannes Beleth's *Rationale divinorum officiorum* (*ca.* 1170).[36] In Beleth's account, Adam sends Seth to Paradise and Seth returns with a branch, which he plants. Solomon uses this tree, which was unsuitable for building the Temple, as a bridge. The Queen of Sheba, adoring the bridge, would not walk upon it. We have here in the Queen of Sheba's refusal to walk upon the wood the reappearance of the tradition which we observed in the *De imagine mundi* version. There is another form of the combined legends which also reveals traces of a number of different influences.[37] It resembles the Beleth version in that Seth and Eve go to Paradise for the oil of mercy, but they receive instead of the oil, a branch. This version resembles the Bodleian and the *Historia* in that the branch has three leaves. And, as in the *De imagine mundi* version, Adam was buried at Calvary. The only new element is the detail that the blood of Christ fell upon the skull of Adam.

In these early combined versions the rood-tree legends were of the twig type; at the next stage, the seed type was to prevail. The most highly developed and most widely influential form of the seed type of legend is a Latin text of the thirteenth century, to which Meyer gives the name *Legende*.[38] Its widespread popularity is attested by the considerable number of manuscripts in Latin and the translations and adaptions in most European languages. This *Legende* is a bold and elaborate tale, a fitting climax to the development of the legends of Seth and the Holy Cross. Here several innovations appear which were to become incorporated in almost every subsequent version. There are the withered footsteps which Adam and Eve made when they left Paradise and which Seth used as a guide. There are the three visions which Seth saw in Paradise: the dry tree, the serpent encircling the trunk, and the baby in the summit. There are the three kernels of the tree of knowledge which Seth was given to plant in his father's mouth. The dry footsteps and the dry tree are symbols of sin and death; the baby in the tree and the seeds are symbols of rebirth. The cedar-cypress-pine tree which grew from the kernels, like most of the subsequent motifs, has appeared earlier. The lady, Maximilla, who sits on the wood, is the harlot of the Bodleian version; the Queen of the South who refuses to walk on the bridge is the queen in Beleth's version. The author of the *Legende* has combined the two traditions of the prophesying women. What each has prophesied comes to pass: on the wood whose long history we have followed, the act of Redemption is consummated. The gift of God's mercy which Seth sought has been given. With this analysis of the *Legende* we will bring to a close our study of the development of the legends of Seth and the Holy Cross.

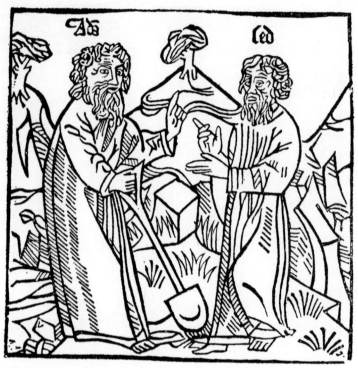

Adam sends Seth to Paradise for some of the Oil of Mercy

Chapter 1

THE QUEST
FOR
THE OIL

The Archangel Michael gives Seth three seeds of the Tree of Life

THE LEGEND of Seth and the Holy Cross consists first of the quest of Seth, an ancient tale whose ultimate origin extends even more remotely into antiquity. Before exploring the earliest beginnings of the Seth story, we might look at the oldest known version.

Authorities are generally agreed that the earliest extant form of the legend of Seth's journey to Paradise is to be found in a work which has been preserved in Greek under the title *The Apocalypse of Moses*. This text seems to have been derived from a Greek translation of an Aramaic original, written by an Alexandrian Jew in the middle or end of the first century A.D. More recently an earlier date has been preferred, between 20 B.C. and A.D. 70.[1] The title, *The Apocalypse of Moses*, has long been recognized as misleading, since the work is neither an apocalypse—a revelation of the future—nor does it concern Moses.[2] It has been variously classified as apocrypha, pseudepigrapha, midrash, and haggada.[3] Since all these terms designate a work, biblical in subject matter, narrative in structure, and edifying in character, any of them would be accurate.

However one describes it, *The Apocalypse of Moses* belongs to a considerable body of extra-canonical literature which developed about Old Testament figures in the first centuries before and after the coming of Christ.[4] Specifically, it describes episodes in the life of Adam and Eve from the time of their expulsion from Paradise to their burial.

The part of *The Apocalypse of Moses* which concerns us here, the journey of Seth to Paradise, may be briefly summarized as follows:

At the age of 930 Adam falls ill and bids all his sons come to him. Seth offers to get the fruit of Paradise, but Adam refuses. Instead he bids Eve and Seth go to Paradise and pray God to give them "of the tree out of which the oil floweth." They are to put earth on their heads, as a sign of penitence. On the way they encounter a wild beast, whose ferocity is dispelled by "the image of God" in Seth. When they arrive, God sends the archangel Michael to refuse Seth "the oil of mercy," but to promise him that it shall be given to the holy people at the end of time.[5]

There are, to my knowledge, no close analogues to this story. But there are certain myths, legends, and apocalypses which offer at one point or another rather striking resemblances to it. We shall, therefore, attempt to isolate the basic elements of the narrative, cite the nearest parallels for each, note differences, and whenever possible account for them.

We might consider the following elements:

16

1. The dying father who sends his son for supernatural aid.
2. The journey to the Earthly Paradise.
3. The supernatural remedy—the oil of mercy.
4. The promise that the righteous shall be rewarded—shall enjoy the tree of life in the world to come.

The motif of the son who seeks a supernatural remedy for the dying father is very widespread. One of the oldest forms of this motif and perhaps the most relevant to this study appears in the Canaanite *Epic of Keret,* composed sometime between 1800 and 1375 B.C.[6] Here the dying father, Keret, summons his son, Elhau, who is instructed to fetch his sister, Thitmanet. Together the son and daughter pour oil into the earth. The god El then fashions an image of loam and sends the goddess Shaʿtaqat to the ailing Keret; she effects his cure.[7]

The parallel between the Seth legend and the Keret legend is basic and obvious: the dying father seeks supernatural aid through his son. But there are significant differences: in *The Epic of Keret* there is no journey to the Earthly Paradise, no promise of eternal life in the hereafter; moreover, a cure is effected, through two rituals—pouring oil into the earth and molding an image of loam into which the malady is transferred.[8]

The precise relationship of the Keret legend to the Seth legend cannot, of course, be determined, but the following points seem clear:

1. There is a basic similarity in situation.
2. There is a possibility of influence (Canaanite influence on Hebrew thought is well established).[9]
3. The differences can be accounted for in either of two ways:
   a) the influence of other stories of the Seth legend,
   b) the characteristic changes which took place in Near Eastern concepts when they were adapted by the Jews.[10]

As we shall see presently, Near Eastern stories may also have influenced the Seth legend at another point, the journey to the Earthly Paradise. The failure of the quest, however, and the substitution of the promise of eternal life in the hereafter are characteristic of Jewish apocalyptic literature which was being produced about the same time as *The Apocalypse of Moses*.[11]

Both legends are concerned with death, though each reflects a different attitude. As Frazer would express it: in the "Age of Magic" men believed that by ritual they could affect the course of natural events (in this case to prolong life); in the "Age of Religion" men accepted the inevitability of death and consoled themselves with the hope of immortality in the hereafter.[12]

Although no proof is possible, it would seem that the Keret legend—or another similar story—may have been known to the Jewish author and may have been adapted by him in the composition of *The Apocalypse of Moses*.[13]

To my knowledge the only other appearance of this motif of the dying father's seeking supernatural aid through the son is in a group of fairy tales known as Grimm No. 97 or Aarne No. 551.[14] Indeed, E. Brugger suggests that the legend of Seth's journey to the Earthly Paradise to get the oil of mercy for his father is a motif borrowed from fairy tale:

> The information we have about the aspect of Terrestrial Paradise after the fall of man is given us by the legend of the holy rood or Seth's journey to Paradise, of which a number of versions are extant. According to this legend, Seth was sent by his father Adam to the cherub guarding Paradise, in order to get from him the *oleum misericordiae* (a motif borrowed from the fairy tale Aarne No. 551; cf. Bolte and Polívka's notes to Grimm No. 97.[15]

Brugger's assumption of the fairy-tale origin of the Seth legend cannot be seriously considered. Brugger himself offers no evidence to support his theory. Further, he does not distinguish between the Seth legend and the legend of the holy rood, which are clearly of separate origin. Although he refers to Meyer's "Die Geschichte des Kreuzholzes vor Christus," he was apparently unfamiliar with Meyer's "*Vita Adae et Evae*," which amply proves the separate origins of the Seth and rood-tree legends and locates the source of the Seth legend in Jewish apocrypha. Finally, the version which he cites is the Latin *Legende*,[16] a late form of the combined Seth and rood-tree legends, a version which represents a long and complex evolution in which no fairy tale influence has been demonstrated.

Still, the basic similarity remains between the initial situations in our legend and in the group of fairy tales known as Aarne No. 551 or Grimm No. 97. There are a number of stories in this group; in each the son—or sons— seeks a marvelous remedy for the ill father. The stories vary principally in details which are not relevant to the Seth legend; a typical version is Grimm's "The Water of Life," which might be briefly summarized as follows:

The eldest prince begs the dying king to be allowed to fetch the water of life, hoping thereby to win his father's favor and kingdom. He meets a dwarf, is discourteous, and is caught in a ravine. The second prince meets the same fate. The youngest, however, is courteous to the dwarf and, after many adventures, is aided by him in drawing the water of life from a spring. Before returning to the king, he rescues his brothers, who proceed to steal the water of life. The two oldest succeed in restoring the king, though after further adventures the youngest is returned to favor and marries the princess.[17]

It is at once apparent that there are very marked differences between the Seth legend and the fairy tale.

1. There are variants in the basic pattern:
   a) There is not one son, but three.
   b) They do not go to the Earthly Paradise.
   c) The remedy is not the oil of mercy, but the water of life; it comes not from the tree of life, but from a spring; moreover, as in the Keret legend, the quest is successful and the king is restored.
2. The additional episodes of each story are entirely different.
3. The theme, purpose, and the tone of each story are differ-

ent. The Seth legend is a story about death; it seeks to show that death came into the world through sin and that only in the hereafter can man enjoy eternal life. It is entirely religious in tone. In the fairy tale the theme is the rivalry of the three brothers; its purpose is to show that through courtesy even the youngest can prevail. The tone is moral but not religious.

The fact that the son's quest for a miraculous cure for his father appears in three very different stories from widely different places and widely different times—modern European fairy tale, ancient Jewish apocrypha, and still more ancient Canaanite legend—suggests one of the following conclusions:

1. Independent origin of all three: For so basic a situation as a sick father's seeking aid through his son, could not one assume independent development, especially as the stories differ so totally in detail and spring from such divergent places and times?

2. Independent development of both the Seth legend and the fairy tale from a common body of ancient stories of which the legend of Keret might be considered representative: In no case can any influence of the fairy tale on the Seth legend be demonstrated; nor is the reverse any more likely. But each has preserved certain primitive elements more faithfully: in the fairy tale the water of life still has the magic power to restore the dying king as the ritual pouring of the oil has the power to restore the dying Keret. In the Seth legend the religious orientation has been preserved, and the theme is the same: man's desire for immortality. As an ancient feature has been preserved by each story, each has been altered to fit the new conditions of its retelling: in the fairy tale the ritual significance has been lost, and the episode is merely one of a series of adventures intended to entertain and to enforce the moral: success comes to the courteous. In the Seth legend the attitude toward immorality is different: there is neither ritual nor remedy which can forestall the inevitability of death; man's only hope is that

through his own righteousness and the grace of God he may win mercy in the hereafter.

The second element of the Seth legend—the journey to the Earthly Paradise—is not present in either *The Epic of Keret* or in "The Water of Life." But we do find it in ancient Babylonian myths and in Jewish apocrypha. Since the older Near Eastern stories offer closer parallels to Seth's journey, we shall consider them first. Of these the most relevant are *The Epic of Gilgamesh*, both the Sumerian version (beginning of the second millennium B.C.) and the Babylonian version (end of the second millennium), and the Akkadian myth of Adapa (fourteenth century B.C.).[18] In each the hero makes a journey to the Earthly Paradise in quest of immortality.[19]

The Sumerian Gilgamesh journeys to the cedar mountain in search of eternal life. In the Babylonian version the journey to the cedar mountain is not connected with the quest for immortality; the quest is postponed to the last episode and is there motivated by the death of the hero's friend, Enkidu.[20] The journey of Gilgamesh in the Babylonian epic more closely resembles that of Seth. The account of the Babylonian hero's journey may be summarized as follows:

After the death of his friend, Enkidu, Gilgamesh sets out to find the secret of eternal life. He arrives at a gate which is guarded by a terrifying pair of scorpion-people. Recognizing his partly divine nature, they permit him to enter. His journey continues across a sea. There he finds Utnapishtim, who has obtained the boon of eternal life. Utnapishtim tells him of a plant which grows on the bottom of the sea and will rejuvenate him who eats it. Gilgamesh gets the plant, but it is devoured by a serpent; Gilgamesh thus obtains and loses the gift of eternal life.[21]

The journey of Gilgamesh differs in many ways from the journey of Seth: difference in motivation (the death of his friend motivates Gilgamesh to seek his own immortality; Seth is motivated by desire to help his sick father); difference in other episodes; different symbol for immortality (plant of life; oil of mercy); different outcome (Gilgamesh gets and loses the plant; Seth receives only a promise). These differences, however, are less striking when one considers that we are dealing with a Babylonian epic of the second millennium B.C. and a Jewish midrash of the first century A.D. As in the case of *The Epic of Keret*, the differences can be accounted for either by the influence of other story patterns or by the changes which the Jews made when they incorporated Near Eastern materials.

The resemblances, though not marked, are worth noting:

1. Similar story pattern: the journey to the other world in quest of immortality.
2. One similar episode: the encounter with an assailant who recognizes the partly divine nature of the hero.
3. Same theme: inevitability of death.

Although proof is not possible, the well-established fact of Babylonian influence on Hebrew culture increases the possibility of a direct connection between the two stories.

Like the epic of Gilgamesh, the Adapa myth involves man's loss of immortality. In some respects Adapa's journey resembles Seth's more closely. Here in brief summary is the relevant part of the Adapa myth:

At the advice of the god Ea, Adapa puts on mourning garb and goes to Heaven to see the god Anu. There at the gate are the gods, Tammuz and Gizzida, who offer him bread and water. He refuses, as he has been told by Ea that these are the bread of death and the water of death. They offer him oil, which he accepts, and he anoints himself. Anu then tells Adapa that it was the bread of life and the water of life which he refused. He has therefore lost the chance for eternal life and must return to the earth.[22]

　　　　　　　　　　　　　　The Quest of Seth

The influence of the Adapa myth on the biblical account of the temptation and fall of Adam has been pointed out.[23] But in certain respects the Adapa myth bears a closer resemblance to the Seth legend:

1. Both heroes are sent on a journey to Paradise (Heaven).
2. Both are instructed to go in mourning garb.
3. Both return to earth without having achieved the object of their quest.

As in the Gilgamesh epic, the differences are at least as conspicuous as the similarities:

1. Adapa does not, like Seth, go for his father.
2. Immortality is symbolized not by the oil of mercy, but by the bread and water of life.
3. The whole pattern of the god, Ea, deceiving the man, Adapa, is absent in the Seth legend.
4. There is no promise given to Adapa.

The differences can, of course, be accounted for by the influence of other stories and the characteristic adaptations made by the Jews.

The motif of the journey to Paradise also occurs in Jewish sources. Both in rabbinic and pseudepigraphic literature a varying number of Old Testament figures enter Paradise alive. Among them are usually Baruch, Moses, and Enoch. Of Baruch we learn that he made a journey to the Five Heavens; of Moses we read that "Gabriel led him to Paradise." More significant is the journey of Enoch to the Earthly Paradise.[24] Enoch's journey, appearing in *1 Enoch* (middle second century or early first century B.C.), was probably the source from which the journeys of Moses and Baruch were derived.[25]

1 Enoch, like the works which relate the journeys of Moses and Baruch, is an "apocalypse"—a work which purports to relate the future. Enoch's journey to the Earthly Paradise is then not so much a journey as a translation. Enoch does not, like Adapa, Gilgamesh, and Seth, go for a supernatural remedy; he is taken to be shown a vision of the future.

It would seem that this second element—the journey to the Earthly Paradise—has very likely been influenced by stories of the hero's quest for immortality, stories such as those of Adapa and Gilgamesh. Although the journey of Enoch does not offer a close analogue to this motif, the work in which it appears, *1 Enoch,* probably did influence the Seth legend in *The Apocalypse of Moses* at other points.

Thus far it would seem that the Keret legend provides the best early analogue for the father's sending the son for the supernatural remedy; the epic of Gilgamesh and the Adapa myth represent clearer analogues for the journey to Paradise. In both the Keret legend and the Adapa myth, oil figures conspicuously. In the epic of Keret, oil is poured into the earth in the ritual healing of the king; in the Adapa myth Adapa is given oil in Heaven and anoints himself. But in neither of them is there any oil of mercy.

The motif of the supernatural remedy is, of course, a commonplace (the water of life in the fairy tales, a plant in the Gilgamesh epic, bread and water in the Adapa myth). The oil of mercy[26] which Seth seeks, however, is different from any of these remedies; indeed, I have been unable to find it mentioned in any earlier source. In none of the reconstructions of the lost Jewish Adam book, which scholars generally agree was the source of *The Apocalypse of Moses,* do we find the oil of mercy. Louis Ginzberg in his two reconstructions suggests that the original might have been "the oil of life" or "the oil of healing";[27] Moses Buttenwieser refers to "the oil of the tree of life."[28] Since neither of these important Jewish scholars believes "the oil of mercy" to have existed in the lost Jewish Adam book, it seems likely that the phrase was coined when the Aramaic version was translated into Greek.[29] No absolute proof is possible, but I hope in the succeeding pages to make the theory seem probable. If this discussion of the oil of mercy seems unduly long, we might bear in mind that it is perhaps the most central and most original concept in the whole episode, that it has no known literary antecedents, that it has reappeared in nearly every succeeding version of the legend, and that its influence has extended to originally unrelated works.[30]

Oil has been regarded in many cultures as a source of life, health, and regeneration. This magical or religious conception of oil seems to be an extension of its general use.[31] The genuine cleansing properties of oil led to its use both as a medicine and to promote a sense of well-being. Its appearance in Babylonian incantations seems to be related to the belief in its curative powers.[32] Probably even more important was the social use of oil in ancient Greece and in the Near East, where it was customary for the host to anoint his guests as a sign of welcome.[33] As Frederic Henry Chase remarks, "by a metaphor drawn from human hospitality, God is said to anoint those whom He regards with favour."[34] References both to the use of oil in healing and to the anointing with holy oil as a sign of God's favor appear frequently in the Old Testament.[35] Here, too, one finds oil used figuratively or symbolically: In Psalm 44:8,[36] "oil of gladness," and in Isaiah 61:3, "oil of joy."

The oil of mercy in the Seth legend is conceived as flowing from a tree, which, as L. S. A. Wells observes, is to be identified with the tree of life.[37] In the mythology of most races and, of course, in the Hebrew Genesis, the tree of life occupies an important place. But there is nothing in Genesis of an oil-producing tree.

We find, however, as part of the ritual-myth of the ancient Sumerians, the anointing of the divine-king with oil from the tree of life. The tree is here identified as the cedar; the oil is cedar oil.[38]

Much closer in time and place to *The Apocalypse of Moses* is the oil-producing tree of life which appears in

2 Enoch. In the A text the tree sends forth oil from its roots; in the B text it discharges the oil of its fruit. To Wells "there is little doubt that the author of the *Apoc. Mos.* is indebted to" *2 Enoch* for his "conception of the Tree of Life and of the sacred oil."[39] Both Wells and Ginzberg assume that the tree in *The Apocalypse of Moses* is, like its counterpart in *2 Enoch,* an olive.[40] It is not, of course, essential for our purpose to identify the species of the tree of life in *The Apocalypse of Moses,* nor even to determine precisely from what source the author derived the concept. We wish merely to point out that there was an ancient and familiar tradition of a tree of life which produced oil—whether cedar, olive, or any other.[41]

Ginzberg notes that this type of tree also played a particularly prominent part in the ritual of the Gnostics, the Ophitic sect in particular.[42] In *Origen against Celsus* there is a reference to anointing with "white ointment from the tree of life."[43] The Gnostic *Recognitions of Clement* refers to God's anointing Christ with oil from the tree of life.[44] These references would be too late to be sources for *The Apocalypse of Moses,* but they bear testimony to the continued currency of the concept. Although the oil-producing tree of life was as old as the rituals of the ancient Sumerians and a standard motif in the milieu of our author, it was probably, as Wells believed, derived from *2 Enoch.*

But what of the concept of mercy or healing? In Ezechiel 47:12 we find that the leaves of the trees in Paradise are for medicine. In the *Apocalypse of Ezra* the fruit of Paradise is used for healing.[45] We have already seen that oil—though not from the tree of life—was used for medication.

In rabbinic literature the concept most resembling the oil of mercy is the "dew of light."[46] Dew as a sign of resurrection appears frequently in Jewish legends,[47] and at least once in the Old Testament.[48] This dew reappears in Jewish apocryphal works[49] and is there connected with oil: in *2 Enoch* 6:1 the dew is "like oil of olive" and in

2 *Enoch* 22:9 the "oil is better than great light and its ointment is like sweet dew."[50]

It seems that all these lines converged: oil used for anointing and healing, the figurative use of oil, oil which flows from the tree of life, the belief that the leaves and fruit of the tree of life are for healing, and the concept of the dew of resurrection and its being compared to oil. These religious and literary concepts were probably quite familiar to the Alexandrian Jew who translated the Aramaic version of *The Apocalypse of Moses* into Greek. Might he not have been sufficiently arrested by the wordplay in Greek between oil (ἔλαιον or ἔλαιος) and mercy (ἔλεος) to coin the phrase, oil of mercy?[51]

The final element, the promise that the tree of life shall be given to the righteous in the world to come, has appeared in no analogue which we have considered; neither has it any biblical antecedent: in Genesis 3:22–24 God casts Adam out of Paradise lest he eat of the tree of life and places at the gates three cherubim and a flaming sword. Although the promise does not appear in the Old Testament, it is a typical apocryphal elaboration on a biblical story. In an earlier episode of *The Apocalypse of Moses*, when Adam asks for the tree of life, God tells him that if he keeps himself from evil, it shall be given to him at the Resurrection.[52] In *1 Enoch* the tree of life at the great judgment "shall be given to the righteous and holy."[53] In the *Testament of Levi* "he [the Messiah] shall open the gates of paradise, and shall remove the threatening sword against Adam. And he shall give to the saints to eat of the tree of life."[54]

In *The Apocalypse of Moses* it is the archangel Michael whom God sends to give Seth the promise. Michael is here performing but one of a number of functions which he performs in the work: in the beginning after Cain murdered Abel, it is he who promises Adam another son, Seth;[55] at the Fall it is he who issues God's judgment of Adam,[56] and hence it is he who most appropriately issues the promise. Michael occupies a similar place in other apocryphal works, especially in *1 Enoch* where he gives the promise of the tree of life, as he does in *The Apocalypse of Moses*.[57] Michael is the angel of mercy: in *1 Enoch* he is called "the merciful," and it is he who shows Enoch "the secrets of mercy."[58] In *3 Baruch* he actually brings oil to the righteous.[59]

Michael's promise that the righteous shall enjoy the tree of life in the hereafter seems then to have been derived from the apocalyptic literature which was being written slightly earlier and at about the same time as *The Apocalypse of Moses*. It is the most characteristically Jewish element of the story. It is on this point that *The Apocalypse* differs so markedly from the earlier Near Eastern analogues which we have considered. Although K. Kohler attributes apocalyptic literature "to circles remote from the seat of Pharisaic or Soferic Judaism,"[60] still this literature bears the higher ethical stamp of Hebraism and more particularly reflects the troubled but hopeful spirit of the Jew in the years preceding and following the advent of Christianity.[61] To the Jew of this era death was inevitable: it was the inescapable consequence of the Fall of Man. The bitterness of death was mitigated only by the promise of life in the hereafter.

Thus far it seems that although the narrative of Seth's journey may have been influenced by ancient Near Eastern stories, the theology is distinctly that of the Hebrew apocalypses. We have now to determine why it was that Seth—a character who is only briefly mentioned in the Old Testament—was the protagonist.

As we observed earlier, it is not uncommon to find that, when canonical records are most sparse, the creators of apocrypha are most prodigal. Given almost nothing but the position as eldest living son of Adam (Cain, of course, excepted), Seth emerged into a full-fledged apocryphal hero. Although it is impossible to trace the exact process by which this development took place, Eastern lore again

The Quest of Seth

seems to have had some influence. According to Angelo S. Rappoport, there are legends of Seth preserved in talmudic and midrashic lore which may be traced to Egypt. The connecting link here probably is the fact that Seth was also the name of an Egyptian sun deity.[62] We cannot know precisely the stages by which Seth developed from a biblical reference into a cult hero, but we know that he became the focal point of a heretical Jewish sect called the Sethites and that he was "the ostensible author of many Gnostic books."[63]

Apart from or related to this tradition—exactly how, it is difficult to determine—there was another tradition which seems to have contributed to the glorification of Seth. We have already had occasion to see that Enoch had become the center of an apocryphal literature and that the Seth legend in *The Apocalypse of Moses* has been influenced by *1* and *2 Enoch*. On this last point, too, the influence of the Enoch literature upon the Seth legend is apparent. The references to Enoch in the Scriptures are as meager as those to Seth, but they are more suggestive of his later position as an apocryphal hero. Of him it is written in Genesis 5:24, "he walked with God, and was seen no more: because God took him." How early this passage became expanded into an Enoch legend is not known. The earliest extant Book of Enoch is an Ethiopic translation of a lost Greek version, which in turn was probably derived from an Aramaic original, variously dated from 170 B.C. to *ca.* 95 B.C.[64] Here Enoch's vision of his journey to Paradise is described, and, as in *The Apocalypse of Moses*, Michael answers the hero's inquiries and gives the promise of the tree of life in the world to come.[65] Gayley, observing the similarity in function between Enoch in *1 Enoch* and Seth in *The Apocalypse*, concludes that "in the capricious favouritism of popular myth-making the apocalyptic adventures of the superhuman Enoch were in time transferred to Seth."[66]

The link between Seth and Enoch is even more closely

established in a passage which Montague Rhodes James quotes from Georgius Syncellus and Georgius Cedrenus. According to James, the passage may preserve a notice of a lost writing under Seth's name: "Seth was caught away by an angel and instructed in what concerned the future."[67] James and R. H. Charles, as well as Gayley, are of the opinion that this is an attempt to transfer to Seth the wisdom and position which belonged to Enoch.[68]

There is further evidence to link Enoch and Seth: Ginzberg cites two traditions concerning the burial of Adam—one in which Enoch buries him and the other in which Seth attends to his funeral.[69] This fusion of Seth and Enoch was very likely aided by the fact that Seth's son was called Enos.

It would seem that the characters of Seth and Enoch fused; the name Seth prevailed, but in some measure the role was that of the apocryphal Enoch.[70]

1 Enoch and *The Apocalypse of Moses* are of different genres: *1 Enoch* is an apocalypse, and the misnamed *Apocalypse of Moses* is a midrash; they are, therefore, different in innumerable ways. But the influence of the Enoch legend on the Seth legend seems probable at the following points: the journey to Paradise, the oil from the tree of life, the promise of reward in the life to come, and Seth as hero. How much these similarities can be attributed to direct influence and how much to the fact that both works sprang from similar conditions cannot be precisely determined. But it seems clear that one of the chief influences shaping the Seth episode in *The Apocalypse of Moses* was Jewish apocryphal literature, especially that which developed about Enoch.

Neither *1 Enoch* nor any other of these extant apocrypha preserves a story pattern which closely resembles that of *The Apocalypse of Moses*. The Alexandrian author may have drawn upon current Near Eastern myths and legends for the narrative; stories resembling the extant Keret legend, the epic of Gilgamesh, and the myth of Adapa would

The Quest of Seth

almost certainly have been familiar. These works or others like them seem to have influenced the form of the basic narrative. But whatever has been borrowed from foreign sources has been transformed so that the work finally emerges as entirely Jewish in character and tone, having a quality similar but not identical to the apocalypses produced previously and at about the same time. Although the sometimes bizarre apocalypses have received far more scholarly attention than the simple midrash,[71] it was the latter which was to become the focal point of the highly developed and widely spread legend which is the subject of this study.

The Greek form of the Seth legend appearing in *The Apocalypse of Moses* is paralleled by a Latin version appearing in the *Vita Adae et Evae*. Both Wells and Meyer consider the *Vita* the later document, belonging most probably to the early fourth century.[72]

There are also somewhat similar versions in Armenian and Slavonic, but since these are most relevant in connection with the rood-tree legend, they will be discussed later.[73] It was the Latin form of the legend which was Christianized, first by the inclusion of material from *The Gospel of Nicodemus* and then by the interpolation of rood-tree material. We shall, therefore, consider briefly the relationship between the Greek and Latin versions.

The Latin *Vita* is somewhat longer than the Greek *Apocalypse*, the *Vita* having fifty-one sections, *The Apocalypse*, forty-three. About one-half of each resembles the other. It seems probable, as Meyer assumes, that both go back to the same original.[74] Scholars differ in their views on which book preserves the ultimate source more faithfully. Meyer believes that the Latin is not only the fuller text but the truer representative of the original.[75] Wells believes that the Greek is the main narrative, to which separate pieces have been attached in the Latin.[76] Fortunately our argument does not depend on the solution of this problem.

The first episode of the *Vita*, the penance of Adam and Eve after their expulsion from Paradise, is not present in *The Apocalypse*.[77] The Seth legend begins with Section XXX and proceeds very much like the narrative in *The Apocalypse*.[78] There is only one difference to be noted between the Seth legend in the Greek and Latin versions, a difference which at first seems trivial but proved of crucial significance in the evolution of the legend. In *The Apocalypse* Adam had taken with him, when he was expelled from Paradise, nard, crocus, calamus, and cinnamon.[79] In the *Vita* Eve and Seth return with these herbs after Michael's prophecy.[80] Their return with the herbs—not even an addition, only a shift in material—provided a sort of substitute for the oil of mercy which they did not get and suggested to future compilers the insertion of the rood-tree material. This development—the joining of the Seth and the rood-tree legends—will be considered after we have discussed the intermediate step, the Christian adoption of the Seth legend.

The first Christianized form of Seth's journey appears in *The Gospel of Nicodemus*. It was the interpolation of part of *The Gospel* into the *Vita* which set in motion the evolution of the legend of Seth and the Holy Cross.

Seth buries Adam and puts the three seeds of the Tree
of Life under his tongue

Chapter 2

THE PROMISE
OF
THE OIL

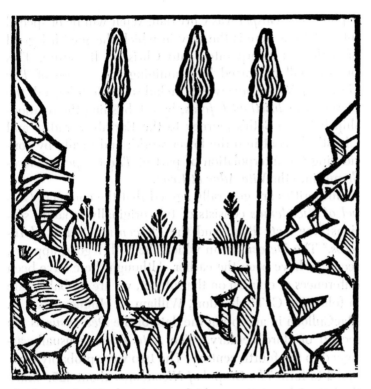

The three seeds spring up

AFTER ITS appearance in the Greek and Latin versions of the Hebrew Adambook, the legend of Seth's journey to Paradise next appears in *The Gospel of Nicodemus*, originally composed in Greek and extant in both Greek and Latin.[1] Like *The Apocalypse of Moses* from which the Seth story was taken, *The Gospel of Nicodemus* is an apocryphal work, stemming from curiosity about gaps in Scriptural narrative: *The Apocalypse of Moses* was concerned with events between the expulsion of Adam and Eve from Paradise and their death; *The Gospel of Nicodemus* dealt with an event between Christ's death and resurrection—his descent into Hell. But *The Apocalypse* was a Jewish apocryphon; *The Gospel* was Christian. What will be of special interest to us here is the way in which the Jewish legend of Seth was incorporated into Christian literature. This process will be traced by examining the section of *The Gospel of Nicodemus* which includes the Seth legend, the *Descensus Christi ad Inferos;* by establishing the relationship between Seth's journey to the Earthly Paradise and Christ's descent into the lower world; and finally by considering the interpolation of part of *The Gospel of Nicodemus* into the *Vita Adae et Evae.*

Authorities are generally agreed that the complete *Gospel of Nicodemus* consists of two originally separate sections: the *Acta Pilati* and the *Descensus Christi ad Inferos.*[2] The *Descensus,* in which the Seth legend appears, seems to have been the earlier. Although there have been differences of opinion on the subject, we are probably safe in following C. Tischendorf, William H. Hulme, and J. A. MacCulloch in accepting the date of the *Descensus* as the second or third century.[3] The *Acta Pilati* is usually assigned to the fourth century. The two were probably combined to form *The Gospel of Nicodemus* about 425.[4] Since the *Vita Adae et Evae,* which contains the Christian adaptation of the Seth legend from the *Descensus,* has been dated fourth century, Seth's story was probably incorporated into the *Descensus* before it was combined with the *Acta Pilati.*[5]

As for the authorship of the *Descensus,* Tischendorf believed it to have been written by a Christian of Jewish origin, well versed in Jewish theology and familiar with Gnostic ideas.[6] A number of authorities have gone even further and identified the author as a certain Lucius Charinus, a writer of apocryphal treatises, who has been variously placed in the second and in the fourth century. But, since the case for his authorship is so uncertain and its relevance to this study so slight, we might assume, as Tischendorf does, that the author of the *Descensus* was an

The Quest of Seth

unidentified Christian of Jewish origin who was familiar with Gnostic ideas.[7]

Closely related to the problem of authorship is the possible Gnostic origin of the work. This issue, too, has occasioned much debate: the Gnostic nature of the *Descensus* is asserted by Richard Adelbert Lipsius[8] and denied by Adolf Harnack.[9] MacCulloch reconciles the divergent viewpoints by stating that the *Descensus* stems from "that widely extended borderline between orthodoxy and Gnosticism, in which beliefs common to both flourished."[10] It seems fairly clear that the work is basically Christian in character. But it is not clear whether this Christian character is to be accounted for by postulating a Christian author, familiar with Gnostic beliefs and not unwilling to incorporate them into his legend, or by assuming that the work represents a Christian revision of a Gnostic writing.[11]

The central event of the *Descensus* is Christ's descent into Hell to free the Old Testament patriarchs. The descent into the lower world, even more than the journey to Paradise, is a theme which has figured largely in the literatures of many peoples, for example, the Babylonians, Egyptians, and Greeks.[12] Among the Jews there existed a belief in the rescue of the patriarchs from Sheol, and in the Old Testament as well as in apocalyptic writings, God appears as a conqueror of the lower world.[13] In the New Testament we read in Ephesians 4:9 that "he [Christ] descended . . . into the lower part of the earth." This passage, together with other similar New Testament passages, formed the basis of the belief that Christ had in truth descended into Hell.[14] As Hulme points out, the verses from the New Testament became the texts for numerous homilies by the early Church Fathers, and they were thus developed and enlarged upon, until we have the *Descensus* in outline in the sermons of Clement of Alexandria and others.[15] The belief in Christ's descent into Hell, which had existed in the church from apostolic times, was later formally recognized as an article of faith. At the Synod of

Sirmium (A.D. 359) the clause, "he descended into Hades," was included in the Apostles' Creed.[16] Although the account in the *Descensus* is apocryphal, the fact that Christians believed Christ to have descended into Hell is surely responsible in part for the enormous popularity of the work. Further, as MacCulloch says, the *Descensus* is "a complete and effective narrative . . . well conceived, skilfully told."[17] We have then the combined appeal of a mythological pattern, an accepted belief, and literary effectiveness. These qualities contributed to the widespread popularity of the *Descensus,* a popularity which is significant to us because in this form the Seth legend became widely known.

Although the *Descensus* was originally written in Greek, the extant Greek manuscripts are later than the earliest written in Latin.[18] The Greek and Latin texts are closely related. At only one point does there seem to be a difference which is significant for the evolution of the Seth legend; this difference will be discussed in another connection. It is the earliest Latin version which will be used as we consider the way in which the Seth story was incorporated into Christian literature.

In the *Descensus* the Seth legend forms, somewhat as in *The Apocalypse of Moses,* a portion of a larger work. But in *The Apocalypse* the Seth story was an integral part of the Adam and Eve story; in the *Descensus* it is a separate narrative, recounted by Seth, and not essentially related to the main pattern. Although the story of Seth's journey to Paradise, inserted in an account of Christ's descent into Hell, seems at first intrusive, it has a certain relevance, not chronological, but structural and theological.

For instance, the two stories are basically parallel: each relates the hero's journey to the other world. But the purpose and outcome are different. Seth's journey begins as a quest and ends with a promise; Christ's mission is the fulfilment of both the quest and the promise. Christ, in his descent into Hell, delivers to Adam the remedy which

The Quest of Seth

Seth, in his journey to Paradise, set out to fetch—the oil of mercy. Although of independent development, the *Descensus* narrative forms both a parallel and a conclusion to the Seth legend.

Before attempting to determine more precisely the relationship between the two stories, we should consider at what point in the *Descensus* narrative Seth's journey has been introduced. In chapter 19, after Christ has descended into Hell, John the Baptist describes Christ's baptism in the Jordan. Adam then bids Seth tell of his journey to Paradise for "the oil of the tree of mercy" and of the promise he was given by the archangel Michael. Seth relates in the first person an abridged form of the story which appears in *The Apocalypse of Moses*. We have here the establishment of two essential connections: first, between the Descent and baptism and, second, between baptism and the Seth story. These connections are the key to the relationship between the two narratives.

The crucial difference between the Seth story in *The Apocalypse of Moses* and in the *Descensus* is Michael's answer to Seth. In place of the general promise that the tree of life shall be given to the righteous in the world to come is the specific promise that in 5,500 years the Son of God shall anoint Adam with the oil of mercy. This promise belongs to a special type of prophecy, extremely common in early Christian and medieval literature, in which the "prophecies" were written long after the events prophesied. Frequently, as here, a foreknowledge of Christ's mission was attributed to Old Testament figures. The device was evidently intended to demonstrate that the two testaments were in harmony, that the New Testament was the fulfilment of the Old, and that Old Testament patriarchs were aware of the New Dispensation which was to come. So Michael was to have announced to Seth: when 5,500 years are accomplished, the Son of God shall raise Adam and baptize him in the Jordan. After he is baptized, he shall be anointed with "the oil of mercy." Then shall the Son bring Adam to Paradise to "the tree of mercy."[19]

We might consider the following new elements, all of which are contained in Michael's prophecy:

1. The promise is to be fulfilled with the coming of Christ.
2. This is to take place in 5,500 years.
3. At that time the Messiah shall baptize Adam in the Jordan.
4. The Messiah shall anoint Adam with the oil of mercy.
5. Finally, the Messiah shall restore Adam to Paradise and give him the tree of mercy.

The first element, that Christ was to redeem Adam, was the most significant innovation: it is the key concept of the *Descensus* version of the Seth legend and recurs in all subsequent versions. In the doctrine of Christ the Redeemer, the author established the relationship of the two stories: Adam who longed for redemption and Christ who had come to redeem. The oil of mercy for which Adam yearned was to be granted by the Messiah whose Advent betokened the gift of God's mercy. To Christians, thinking of Old Testament persons and events as prefigurations of those in the New Testament, the Seth story must have borne a prefigurative relationship to Christ's coming.[20]

The period of 5,500 years, which was to elapse between the death of Adam and the death of Christ, was established during the early centuries as the interval between the Creation and Incarnation. The figure was based on the belief that as the Creation was completed in six days, and as "one day with the Lord is as a thousand years,"[21] the consummation of all things was to be achieved in 6,000 years. The Incarnation was to have taken place in the middle of the last millennium, that is, 5,500 years after Adam's death.[22] The round figure 5,500 was used by the author of the *Descensus,* not for the birth of Christ, but for his descent into Hell.

It was here that Christ was to bring Adam the long-awaited oil of mercy. But first Adam was to be baptized.

As Christ himself said, "Unless a man be born again of water and the Holy Ghost, he cannot enter into the kingdom of God" (John 3:5). It was thus in the sacrament of baptism that the author found for Adam his entrance into eternal life.[23] Christ's redemption of man from original sin by baptism was, of course, orthodox Christian doctrine. The actual relationship, moreover, between the two beliefs—Christ's ministry in Hell and the efficacy of baptism—was not new in the *Descensus*.[24] The two beliefs were, as J. H. Bernard points out, associated in the New Testament, an association which recurred in many early Christian writers.[25] The beliefs were, according to Bernard, viewed as antitypal in the early church, that is, the Descent was the type or pattern of which baptism was the antitype.[26] Bernard has further sought to show that the ultimate relationship between the two ideas stems from the belief that both baptism and Christ's mission in Hell involved the descent into the water of the primeval abyss.[27]

In none of the sources which Bernard cites as relating baptism and the Descent does Christ actually baptize Adam. As far as I am aware, the only other appearance of this element may be in Manichaean literature. Theodor bar Kōnay, the Nestorian bishop of Kashkar (lower Babylonia), in his *Book of Scholia* (Syriac, sixth or seventh century), quoted directly from a Manichaean writing in which Christ awakens Adam, baptizes him, and gives him to eat of the tree of life.[28] Although it does not seem to be explicitly stated in early Christian literature that Christ baptized Adam, it is implicit in the *Epistle of the Apostles* (written about 160) where Christ, speaking of his Descent, tells of baptizing the righteous dead.[29]

The additional detail in the *Descensus* that Adam should be baptized in the Jordan was appropriate: it was in the Jordan that John the Baptist began baptizing, and it was here that Christ himself had been baptized.[30] Indeed, it was during John's account of Christ's baptism in the Jordan that Adam prompted Seth to relate his story. The relationship between the Descent and baptism is then of crucial significance, for it was probably the oil used in baptism which suggested to the author of the *Descensus* Seth's story of his quest for the oil.

Following his immersion, Adam is to be anointed.[31] According to MacCulloch, "the anointing with the oil of mercy from the tree in *Nicodemus* is obviously connected with the use of oil in baptism."[32] It is not apparent, however, precisely what this connection is, and MacCulloch does not explain. Does he intend to suggest that it was the association of the oil of mercy and the oil used in baptism which led to the inclusion of the Seth story? Or does he consider the anointing with the oil of mercy to be a part of the baptismal rite? Both interpretations are based on the assumption that anointing was a part of baptism at the time the *Descensus* was written (second or third century), an assumption which seems entirely justified. For instance, before the end of the second century Tertullian mentioned the use of oil in baptism.[33] The first of these possibilities—that the author of the *Descensus* was led to incorporate the Seth story into his narrative by his associating the two oils—is, as we suggested earlier, very likely. The remaining possibility, that the anointing of Adam was intended as a part of his baptism, seems less probable. First, the two acts are described as quite separate. Further, the anointing is to follow, not to precede, the actual baptism, as is the custom in Catholic baptism. This latter point, however, is negligable, since there is evidence that the present form of the baptismal rite was not established until the third century and that prior to this time anointing sometimes followed immersion.[34] In Tertullian, for example, the earliest source for the use of oil in baptism, immersion preceded anointing.[35]

Although at the time the *Descensus* was written, anointing might have followed immersion, still it seems more probable that Adam's receiving the oil of mercy was not intended in the *Descensus* to be a part of the baptismal rite; it was to be a separate act, the literal fulfilment of Adam's request. The anointing bears a parallel relation to the immersion. Both the water and the oil convey the same significance: mercy, or the forgiveness of sin. The oil of mercy which Seth sought was probably interpreted as a prefiguration of the oil used in baptism. Seth's story has been included then, not in its full significance, nor blended into the Christian retelling, but narrated in brief, that is, presented as a type of the more significant event, the Descent, which was itself considered a type of the Christian sacrament of baptism.

Finally, after Adam has been baptized and anointed with the oil of mercy, he is to be led by Christ to Paradise and there given "the tree of mercy." The closest parallel to this element is in the Manichaean writing which we cited earlier in connection with Christ's baptism of Adam. Here, after baptism, Christ gives Adam to eat of the tree of life.[36] In the *Descensus* the tree is called the tree of mercy, but it is evidently the tree of life, and the change was made to link it to the oil of mercy. The addition of entrance into Paradise fulfils more completely the cycle of fall and redemption. The significance of this final act seems the same as the preceding two: the baptism, the anointing with the oil of mercy, and the bestowal of the tree of mercy—all represent the forgiveness of sin and the restoration to divine favor.[37]

The use of these two sources or traditions, *The Apocalypse of Moses* and the Manichaean work, has led to an agglomeration of motifs which, though not inconsistent, are repetitious. The anointing of Adam and his restoration to Paradise form a fitting conclusion to the Seth legend; the bestowal of the tree of mercy adds nothing, however, and the inclusion of baptism serves chiefly to imbed the narrative in Christian doctrine.

The author of the *Descensus* seems most forcefully impressed with the concept of Christ the Redeemer, who instituted the sacrament of baptism, and Christ the Harrower of Hell, who led forth the patriarchs to Paradise. We have here a recognition of the close parallel between baptism, the sacrament of rebirth, and the descent into the earth, as part of the drama of rebirth. The Seth legend was perceived as relevant to this theme in that the fulfilment of Seth's quest for the oil of mercy was to be found in the anointing at baptism. But the legend has not been fully incorporated into its new setting;[38] it provides in the *Descensus* only a narrative interlude, linked to the main body of the story by the doctrine of the redemptive power of Christ. He is the second Adam who has come to free the first Adam of the consequences of original sin. Christ's redemptive act here consists of four parts: baptism, the bestowal of the oil of mercy, the admission into Paradise, and the granting of the tree of eternal life. In terms of the drama of the *Descensus* the insertion of Seth's story added little, but in terms of the evolution of the Seth legend, our principal concern, its insertion was fortunate. For the Seth legend had become incorporated into Christian legend, a Christian legend which was to enjoy great popularity and hence was to give currency to Seth's account of his journey.

From the fifth century on, after its translation from Greek into Latin, the *Descensus* version of the Seth legend became widely dispersed, as is attested by numerous manuscripts both in Latin and in the vernacular.[39] But since it is not primarily the dispersal of the Seth legend but its evolution which interests us, we shall make no attempt to trace the spread of the legend in this early form. We might note only that the *Descensus* proved especially popular in England, appearing in the Latin version not long after Christianity began to flourish there.[40]

So we have in the *Descensus* Seth's story, incorporated into Christian legend, but reduced in size and placed in an unpromising setting. This handling was not detrimental,

The Quest of Seth

however, for the Seth legend was shortly to resume an independent form, retaining from the *Descensus* only its Christianization. This next stage in the evolution of our legend is represented by the interpolation of the prophecy into the fourth-century Latin *Vita Adae et Evae*. In it we find a reversal of the situation which we have seen in the *Descensus*. Instead of a Christian work into which an abridged form of the Seth legend has been inserted, we have the original Seth legend in which the Christian addition has been interpolated.

The insertion of material from *The Gospel of Nicodemus* into the *Vita* occurs at the point at which Michael refuses Seth and Eve the oil of mercy. He gives them instead the prophecy of Christ's coming. It is not certain when the interpolation was made, but it appears in the earliest manuscript of the *Vita* (eighth century).[41]

As *The Gospel of Nicodemus* version of the Seth legend is interpolated into the *Vita*, certain changes occur: the idea of Christ's descent into Hell is obscured; Michael announces that Christ will come upon earth to revive the body of Adam, that He will be baptized in the Jordan and will anoint with the oil of mercy all those who have been baptized. Then Christ will lead Adam to Paradise and to the tree of mercy. Christ as the bringer of the oil of mercy was retained from *The Gospel of Nicodemus*, but Christ as the Harrower of Hell was dropped and was of no further significance in the evolving Seth legend. The anointing with the oil of mercy seems to have been incorporated into the rite of baptism.

The inclusion in the *Vita* of the prophecy from *The Gospel of Nicodemus* marked the beginning of the Christianizing process. But in relating Adam's salvation to baptism, only the first step was taken. For baptism does not constitute redemption. It is the sacrifice of Christ on the cross which redeemed man from the consequences of original sin; the efficacy of baptism depends on the Crucifixion. The next step was to relate Seth's journey and the Crucifixion, the central event in Christian worship. As previously oil was the link and the symbol connecting the Seth legend and Christianity, in the next phase it is wood which becomes the link and the symbol: into the *Vita* was interpolated an account of Seth's returning from Paradise with a twig which was to become the wood of the cross.

It remains for us to consider the origin of the rood-tree legend and the way in which the rood-tree and Seth legends were merged.

Moses always has the three rods with him

Chapter 3

THE DISCOVERY
OF
THE TWIGS

David leaves the rods for the night

WE HAVE traced the story of Seth's journey to Paradise from its origin in Jewish apocrypha to its inclusion in Christian legend. The next stage in the evolution of the story is its amalgamation into a complex of legends centered upon the cross.

To the medieval Christian, the cross on which the Savior died for the redemption of man was made of no ordinary wood. Following Saint Helena's discovery of the rood-tree, fragments had been dispersed throughout Christendom and had become objects of veneration and speculation. From those two impulses of the medieval imagination, curiosity and credulity, a body of legend developed about the wood of the cross.[1] Miracles were attributed to the relics whose wonder-working power was linked not only to the cross but to the marvelous wood of the Old Testament. For instance, in most versions of the legend, the rod of Moses is identified as the very wood of which the cross was made. In some versions the rood-tree first appears at the time of David. In many forms of the legend the wood figures in Solomon's construction of his Temple; in some the wood is traced back to the tree of knowledge in Paradise.

These varying accounts of the origin of the rood-tree appeared in Latin and in the western European languages at approximately the same time—the eleventh and twelfth centuries. The fact that some of these versions were independent of the Seth legend and some were related to it, raises the following questions: first, did the rood-tree legends which were separate from the Seth story have an independent origin, and, if so, what was it; second, if they developed from the Seth legend, how were they separated? Clues leading to the solution of these problems may appear as we examine some of the earlier forms of the rood-tree legend. We shall begin with those which lack the Seth narrative.

Probably the earliest extant legend of this type in the West is the English version which appears in the Bodleian manuscript 343.[2] Not only is the Seth legend lacking here, but, according to its editor, Napier, the account of Seth's journey was also lacking in its ultimate source.[3] Napier estimates that the Bodleian version was a modernized copy of a text belonging to the early eleventh century. A parallel fragment of the mid-eleventh century has since been found which substantiates Napier's belief in the existence of an eleventh-century rood-tree legend in England.[4] Napier further demonstrates that the earlier English form was in turn derived from a Latin source. This version then would antedate by about one hundred years the Latin *Historia* (before 1150), which Meyer considers the earliest of the rood-tree legends.[5] The Bodleian version represents not only an earlier but also, in some respects, a more primitive form.

The narrative opens with these words: "Here begins to be told concerning the tree of which the rood was wrought on which our lord suffered for the salvation of all mankind, how it first began to grow." Then follows the account of how on a spot where Moses once lay there grew three rods: one at his head, a second at his right side, a third at his left. The next day the rods followed him and repeated their pattern. Moses recognized that these rods betokened the Father, the Son, and the Holy Spirit. He took the rods with him and by placing them in a spring changed the bitter water into sweet.

Later David saw the rods burn without being consumed. When he got possession of the rods, he too placed them in water. Again some of the magical properties of the rods were transferred to the water, for with it he restored a man to health. A voice told David that the rods signified the Trinity: cypress, the Father; cedar, the Son; pine, the Holy Spirit. David performed other miracles including the cleansing of a leper with the flaming rods. In Jerusalem the rods could not be moved but grew into a single trunk with three different kinds of branches—cypress, cedar, and pine. Every year for thirty years David put a silver hoop around the tree.

These silver hoops were later taken by Solomon and made into plates, which still later were used by Judas to betray Christ. Solomon's workmen cut down the tree to use in the construction of the Temple, but the tree could not be used as it was always too long or too short. Solomon had the tree placed in the Temple where it remained until the time of the Crucifixion.

Once a harlot sat on the tree, and it burst into flame. She prophesied, "Lo, thou blessed tree, on which the Saviour of the world shall hang!" She was beaten by the Jews and placed in prison where an angel first addressed her as "Sibilla," later as "Susanna." She was put to death for blasphemy.

At the time of the Crucifixion men were unable to move the tree; they cut off a portion which Christ carried from the Temple, and of it the cross was made.

Then after 330 years Saint Helena came to Jerusalem to find the holy rood. The true cross was distinguished from the robber's cross when it restored a dead man to life.[6]

As the first step in our analysis of this complex and highly developed legend, we shall divide the narrative into elements:

1. Moses discovers three rods—one at his head; one at his left side; one at his right side.
2. The rods follow him.
3. Moses recognizes that they betoken the Trinity.
4. With them Moses sweetens the bitter water.
5. David sees the three rods burn without being consumed.
6. With the rods David cleanses the water and restores a man to health.
7. David is told by a voice that the rods represent the Trinity —cypress, the Father; cedar, the Son; pine, the Holy Spirit.
8. David cures a leper with the flaming rods.
9. In Jerusalem the rods cannot be moved.
10. The three rods become one tree with three different kinds of branches—cypress, cedar, and pine.
11. David has a silver hoop made each year for thirty years. (The silver was later used by Judas.)
12. The tree, always too long or too short for use in building Solomon's Temple, is placed inside the Temple.
13. No one can move it; no one can cut it.
14. A harlot sits on the tree; it bursts into flame; she prophesies its use in the Crucifixion. An angel addresses her as Sibilla; later, Susanna.
15. At the time of the Crucifixion the tree is cut, and Christ carries it from the Temple.

Before examining what might be the ultimate source of this narrative, we should consider what Napier says of

The Quest of Seth

sources. He points out that the rood-tree group of legends —to which the Bodleian version belongs—cannot, as Meyer believes, have been derived from the Latin *Legende*.[7] We shall not attempt to summarize Napier's completely convincing arguments but only state his conclusion: the *Legende* and the Bodleian version both go back to a common source. Napier postulates at least three links separating the Bodleian from this unknown common source.[8]

Although it has been assumed that the rood-tree legends are of Greek origin,[9] there have not been, to my knowledge, any close comparisons between Eastern and Western versions. Most valuable in this connection is the material provided by Moses Gaster.[10] He summarizes a "Legend of the Cross," extant in Old Slavonic and based on Greek sources. It was composed about 940, supposedly by the leader of the heretical sect of Bogomils, Popa Jeremiah.[11] According to this version, Satanael planted in Paradise a tree which had three branches: the first branch belonged to Adam; the second, to Eve; the third, to God. Each branch grew into a tree. It is the second part of this legend—the part which deals with the second or Eve's tree —which bears a marked resemblance to the key incidents in the Bodleian version. It is with the root of this second tree that Moses sweetened the waters of Marah.[12] From the same tree Solomon got logs but was unable to use them in building the Temple. On one of these logs "Queen Sivila" sat and was burned. Thus in three central episodes —those involving Moses, Solomon, and Queen Sivila—the Slavonic and English versions are almost identical. The tree with the three branches also appears in both, though in different places: in the Bodleian version the tree grew from the three rods; in the Slavonic both the original tree in Paradise and the third, or God's tree, have three branches. It was of this latter tree that the cross was made.[13]

The close resemblance between these two versions suggests either Slavonic influence on the English or a common origin—probably Greek. Although it is theoretically possible that Western versions influenced Eastern, this view is held by no scholar known to me nor does there seem to be any evidence to support it. The origin of the rood-tree legends in the East is almost certain, but the way in which they were transmitted to the West has not been determined.

Meyer supposes transmission to have taken place through the returning Crusaders.[14] But since the first Crusade did not begin until 1095, this theory cannot account for a highly developed rood-tree legend in English in the middle of the eleventh century.

The theory which Gaster offers provides an interesting possibility. He believes that Slavonic adaptations of Greek versions were transmitted by the Bogomils, the Bulgarian heretical sect whose legend of the cross we have just been discussing. According to Gaster, when they spread into Italy and France, they brought with them legends, incorporated in their vernacular version of the Bible, the Slavonic *Palaea* or *Bible historiale,* dating from the ninth century.[15] It is generally accepted that the influence of the Bogomils is traceable in Italy and particularly in southern France where their ideas had a great impact upon the heretical tenets of the Albigensians.[16] Modern historians, notably Steven Runciman and Dmitri Obolensky,[17] accept the probability of Gaster's theory, but unfortunately, proof is lacking since the Albigensian Crusade destroyed most of the heretical literature. But it would seem that traces of it—cut off from its heretical roots and made orthodox—are present in a number of Italian, French, and Latin texts, as well as in the Bodleian version.[18]

As Gaster indicates, this Slavonic legend was derived from Greek sources. We are fortunate in having a Greek version which, although appearing in a late manuscript (fourteenth or fifteenth century),[19] preserves elements of an early text. In the following respects it may be compared to the Bodleian version:

The Quest of Seth

1. Three sprigs—of pine, cedar, and cypress—were planted apart but grew together in one trunk.
2. The author denies that this was the rod with which the bitter waters were sweetened.
3. The tree proved unfit for use in the construction of the Temple and was placed inside.
4. The Queen of Sheba refused to sit on the tree and prophesied that Christ would die on it.
5. It was decorated with thirty silver rings, which were later given to Judas.

The four elements common to the Slavonic and Bodleian versions are also present in the Greek, though in somewhat altered form. The Greek also contains the episode of David and the silver hoops, present in the Bodleian version, but not in the Slavonic. This placing of silver hoops about the sacred tree is an ancient motif, having formed part of the New Year festivals of the Babylonians.[20] As is so often the case in legend-making, an ancient ritual has reappeared in a totally different context and been given an entirely different interpretation.

Meyer is surely mistaken, as Napier believes, in his theory that this Greek version is derived from the Latin *Legende*;[21] on every point the Greek represents a more primitive form than the *Legende*. Napier believes it to be more ancient than the Bodleian version in every respect, but, as I hope to demonstrate later, the wood which bursts into flame when the harlot sits on it represents the original form of the episode, and the Queen of Sheba who refuses to sit on the holy wood is a link between the early form and the later one which appears in the *Legende* and elsewhere: the Queen of Sheba will not step on the bridge made of the holy wood.

It would seem that there existed at an early period Greek rood-tree legends, similar in some respects to the version we have just considered. It is possible, though less certain, that these Greek versions were translated and adapted by the Bogomils and brought by them to western

Europe. At least, no more probable theory exists to explain the transmission of the legend.

A point which remains to be considered is the abrupt beginning of the Bodleian version: the wood which was to become the cross simply appeared. As we have seen, the Slavonic version ascribes a more ancient origin to the tree: it came from Paradise. Moreover, Seth is included in the complete Slavonic rood-tree legend. Why then, if the Slavonic represents the ultimate source of the Bodleian version, were Seth and the Paradise origin omitted? The answer, I think, lies in the heretical nature of the source: the tree which was to become the cross was planted by Satanael. Perhaps in the Bodleian form of the legend, the first part was cut off to eliminate all possible traces of its heretical origin. As we shall see presently, other adaptations of the heretical material preserved the Seth story and excluded the heresy.

Of the elements present in the English version and not present in either the Slavonic or the Greek, at least one might have developed on the analogy of elements in the Eastern versions. In the Slavonic, the wood lengthens and shortens when it is used to build the Temple, and it bursts into flame when sat on by the harlot. Both of these elements illustrate in a spectacular way the wood's ability to resist being used for an unsuitable purpose.[22] In the Bodleian version the tree also resists being moved or cut until the proper time has come, until it has reached its destined end as the cross.[23] These are ancient elements going back to times when men believed trees to be animate. But here the ancient motifs have been transformed and made to serve a new purpose—to emphasize the importance of the Crucifixion by encouraging a veneration for the wood of the cross.

Although Slavonic sources may account for certain episodes revealing the marvelous power of the tree, other incidents have been added to illustrate the same point. These seem to have been derived from the joining of the rood-tree and Helena legends. Since the latter long ante-dated the former,[24] and since features of the Helena section appear also in the rood-tree section (but in neither the Greek and Slavonic sources nor in other early legends of the cross), it seems probable that the *origo crucis* legend has been adapted to fit the *inventio crucis* legend. The theme of the entire work is the miraculous nature of the wood, from the first appearance of the rods to Moses to the final recovery of the cross by Saint Helena. But the miracles of healing which appear in the *origo crucis* have probably been formed on the basis of one miracle in the *inventio crucis*. At the end of Saint Helena's quest, the true cross is distinguished from the robber's by its restoring a dead man to life.[25] This restorative quality of the wood has been attributed to it in two episodes in which David figures: the rods purify the water, which in turn heals a man, and the rods emit flames, which cure a leper.

The frequency with which the wood bursts into flame is to be observed in both sections. Flames, although an age-old manifestation of the deity, do not appear in other early rood-tree legends, and in the Slavonic version they appear only once. It is possible that in this case it was the *origo crucis* legend which has influenced the *inventio crucis*. It seems entirely possible that from the wood's bursting into flame when the harlot sat on it came the suggestion for the many other instances, in both sections, of the rods bursting into flames.

Another feature characteristic of both parts and possibly derived from the Helena legend is the frequent appearance of voices and visions; they appear to Moses, David, Sibilla, Helena, and Constantine. Although visions are a commonplace in religious literature, the fact that they do not occur in either the Slavonic and Greek sources or early rood-tree versions suggests the influence of the Helena legend.

In the section on the finding of the cross much emphasis is also placed on the doctrine of the Trinity. This emphasis, I would hazard, comes from the *origo crucis* legend. We have seen that the image of the Trinity—the tree with the three kinds of branches—appears in the Slavonic. But the explicit and continuous reference to the Trinity is characteristic of the Bodleian version. For instance, traditionally Moses had one rod, but in the Bodleian version three appear to him.[26] He is informed that they symbolize the Trinity,[27] that the cypress signifies the Father; the cedar, the Son; and the pine, the Holy Spirit. Joining the legend at this point is the tradition that the cross was made of three different kinds of wood. This idea appeared as early as Chrysostom (fourth century), who derived it from his interpretation of Isaiah's prophecy:

> The glory of Lebanon shall come unto thee; the cypress tree, the pine tree and the cedar tree together, to beautify the place of my sanctuary; and I will make the place of my feet glorious.[28]

The concept of the Trinity also underlies the notion that the cross was made of three kinds of wood: in substance as well as in form the cross was believed to symbolize the Trinity.

In the three rods joined into a single trunk with three kinds of branches, both the Trinity and the cross are prefigured. Similarly, the rods which appear at the head and on each side of Moses prefigure the cross and the Trinity. Most of the elements, not present in the Slavonic or Greek rood-tree legends or the Helena legend, emphasize this point, that the great Christian mysteries, the triune nature of God and the Crucifixion, were familiar to representatives of the Old Law.

In the Bodleian version the episodes are grouped around three Old Testament figures—Moses, David, and Solomon. Moses appears in the Slavonic version but not David. It would seem that in the Bodleian legend David has been assigned a portion of the role which earlier belonged to Moses, that he has begun to assume the position of im-

The Quest of Seth

portance which he enjoyed in the West. For instance, there have been transferred to the ancestor of Christ some of the miracles associated with wood which in the Old Testament belong to Moses. The episode of the rods which burn but are not consumed is clearly based on Moses' vision of the burning bush (Exod. 3:2). David, like Moses, is made aware that the rods represent the Trinity. It is while they are in David's possession that they grow together to form the tree with the three kinds of branches. The importance of Moses and David in the drama of the cross becomes more understandable when we realize that Old Testament passages, ascribed to them or chronicling their actions, were interpreted by the Fathers as prophetic or prefigurative of the Crucifixion.[29]

The role of Solomon in the Bodleian version—as in the Slavonic—is different from that of Moses and David: they are intended to show the link between the Old Law and the New Law; Solomon, as the great Jewish king and builder of the Temple, symbolizes Judaism. In his failure to recognize the unique nature and destiny of the wood, he prefigured the failure of the Jews to recognize the Messiah. This point will become clearer in subsequent versions. The inclusion of all three represents an attempt to relate the miraculous wood of the Old Testament (and Old Testament legends) to the wood of the cross.

One of the most complex and not readily explicable episodes of the Bodleian version is one which occurs during Solomon's reign: the harlot sits on the tree, and, when it bursts into flame, she prophesies its use in the Crucifixion. As we have seen, the incident appears in a somewhat abbreviated form in the Slavonic version, but tracing it to another language and an earlier time still leaves it unexplained. One feels that it is essentially a primitive story and that the main point—the power of the wood not only to burst into flames and remain unconsumed but to cleanse and convert the unbeliever—was introduced at a later time. This episode—which is to reappear in all subsequent versions of the rood-tree legend, though in variant forms—warrants closer analysis.

Of key significance is the harlot's later being addressed as "Sibilla." We might, therefore, consider the episode in terms of the sibyl in general, the relationship between the harlot and the sibyl, the sibyl as prophetess, and her relationship to Solomon. "Sibilla" evidently is related to a whole complex of legends which developed about "the sibyl."[30] According to the oldest traditions she was given to oracular utterances. Very early in her career the sibyl acquired a reputation not only for prophetic powers but for sensuality; indeed, the two seem to have been related.[31] Later writers speak of various sibyls in connection with the places where they were said to prophesy. According to Lactantius, there were ten sibyls: the Persian, the Libyan, the Delphian, the Cimmerian, the Erythraean, the Samian, the Cumaean, the Hellespontian, the Phrygian, and the Tiburtine.[32] These were all, of course, pagan sibyls. In the second century B.C. the Alexandrian Jews took advantage of the veneration in which the sibyls were held and ascribed to them verses in which were inserted Jewish doctrines.[33] The Christian writers of the first and second centuries, in turn, in an effort to convert the pagans, ascribed to these sibyls oracles which contained Christian teachings.[34] Among these sibylline oracles written by Christians, was the prophecy which appears at the end of the sixth book of the *Sibylline Oracles,* dated second century by H. C. O. Lanchester.[35] I quote the passage, originally in Greek, in translation:

> O happy wood, on which God was first extended!
> The earth will not hold you, but the temple of heaven
>   will behold you
> When the lighted form of God appears in its splendor.[36]

It is, of course, this prophecy from the sixth book of the *Sibylline Oracles* that the harlot, "Sibilla," utters when the tree bursts into flame.

Her prophecy is delivered to Solomon at his Temple. The presence of Sibilla at the court of Solomon reminds one of the celebrated visit of the Queen of Sheba. There is, moreover, a well-established tradition that the Queen of Sheba and one of the sibyls were merged. This merging of characters is a common occurrence in legend, especially if they possess common traits and similar names. Both the Queen and the sibyls were famed for their wisdom, and among the sibyls was one called Sabbe. Pausanias mentioned her as a Babylonian or Egyptian prophetess living among the Hebrews.[37] It was probably with this sibyl, Sabbe, that the Queen of Sheba (Saba) was first identified. Of the actual merging the earliest conclusive evidence is from the ninth-century world chronicle of the Byzantine monk Georgius. Here the Queen of Sheba is referred to as "Sibylla, Queen of the Ethiopians" (in the title) and "the Queen of Saba . . . called sibyl by the Greeks" (in the narrative which follows).[38] In the Byzantine world of the ninth century the Queen of Sheba and Sibilla were one.[39] The identification of the two women is not as evident in the Bodleian as in other versions, but it provides the basis for explaining Sibilla's appearance at Solomon's Temple.

The essential elements of the Sibilla episode are present in the Slavonic version, but in the Bodleian, the already complicated figure, Sibilla, has been further identified with Susanna.[40] The reason for the conflation of Sibilla and Susanna is not immediately apparent. The names do not resemble each other closely, nor do the characters or their stories. The only points of resemblance seem to be that a tree figures in both episodes and that both women are associated with illicit love: Sibilla is a harlot and Susanna is accused of adultery. This latter point, I believe, is the clue to the linking of the two women. The emergence of the harlot, Sibilla, from the flaming wood may have reminded the author of stories current in the Middle Ages of women accused of adultery who were condemned to be burned or required to submit to a trial by fire and who miraculously survived the flames.[41] These may in turn have suggested Susanna's deliverance from the false accusation of infidelity. For whatever reason, the harlot-sibyl in the Bodleian version is finally addressed as Susanna. Once the identification was made, certain changes took place in the Sibilla episode. Among the most striking is the persecution of the harlot, Sibilla-Susanna, by the Jewish priests. She emerged safely from the burning wood, only to be condemned to death, not, however, for infidelity to an old husband, but for infidelity to the Old Law. She was the first to die for Christ; she was a pre-Christian martyr.

As we conclude our analysis of the Bodleian version, it is still not possible to answer with certainty the key question raised in this chapter: what is the origin of the rood-tree legend? But thus far it seems probable that the Bodleian version and its English and Latin sources are truncated adaptations of a fully developed legend whose heretical beginning has been omitted. This point will be clearer when we examine the fusion of the Seth and rood-tree legends, for here it would seem that another part of the Eastern version has been separated from its heretical roots and joined to the Christianized *Vita*. Further evidence will be provided to support a thesis which, I believe, is already established: the Greek origin of the rood-tree legends.

There is one other early form of the rood-tree legend, the Latin *Historia*. Printed by Meyer and dated by him before 1150, it bears the following title, "De ligno crucis, quod in antiquis libris est repertum."[42]

In some respects the Bodleian version resembles the Slavonic more closely than the *Historia* does, but the Bodleian contains a far larger number of additions than the *Historia*. Before considering the relationship between the two Western versions and between the Latin and

Slavonic, we should examine the *Historia* in detail. In a somewhat abridged form the narrative is as follows:

A certain Jew, finding a tree which bore three kinds of leaves, brought it to King David. When the king saw the tree, he honored it for he realized its significance. The tree was likewise venerated by Solomon, who gilded it. When the Queen of the South came to visit him, however, she said that if Solomon knew what the wood signified, he would by no means adore it. Later the Queen prophesied that on this tree would die one who would bring about the downfall of the Jews. When Solomon learned of this prophecy, he stripped the tree of its gold and hurled it into a fishpond. From then on an angel descended daily into the pond, and as he searched for the wood, the movement of the water caused the sick who bathed there to be cured. As the time of the Passion of Christ drew near, the pond dried up and the wood was taken to form the cross on which Christ was crucified.

This version may be considered in terms of the following elements:

1. A tree with three kinds of leaves is found.
2. It is honored by David.
3. It is honored by Solomon, who gilds it.
4. The Queen of the South visits Solomon and prophesies that one will die on this tree who will bring about the downfall of the Jews.
5. Solomon strips the tree of its gold and hurls it into a fishpond, where, as an angel descends to search for it, healings are performed.
6. It becomes the wood of the cross.

The tree with the three kinds of leaves has been discussed: we observed its appearance in the Bodleian version and considered the possibility of its origin in Slavonic sources.[43] But in the *Historia* it first appears not to Moses, but to David. We have seen in the Bodleian version how David began to assume the role which in the Slavonic had belonged entirely to Moses. The process of dissociating Moses, the representative of the Old Law, and the mar-

velous tree is here complete: the honor has been trans-
ferred to David, the ancestor of Christ. On this point, the
Historia differs more from the Slavonic version than the
Bodleian does.

The next difference which we notice is the absence of
the episode in which Solomon attempts to use the tree in
building his Temple. This episode of the lengthening and
shortening of the tree—present in the Greek, Slavonic, and
English versions—may have been discarded by the redactor or his source as unbecoming to the high destiny of the
holy wood. It is also possible that the *Historia* was drawn
from sources which did not contain this incident. In any
case, its omission tends to preserve the dignified tone of
the narrative.

The omission of the incident in which the wood is cut
down for the Temple results in a further difference: the
tree is still growing at the time of the Queen's visit.

Also, Solomon honors the tree by gilding it, not encircling it with silver bands, as in the English form of the
legend. These bands appeared in the Greek version, but
not in the Slavonic. The decorating with gold or silver may
represent parallel traditions; it is difficult to determine at
this point which—if either—was the original. There is, of
course, a well-established biblical tradition of Solomon's
gilding activities: in III Kings 6 he gilded the oracle, the
cherubim, the doors of the house, and the floor of the
house within and without! The gilding of the tree would
seem to indicate Old Testament influence.

The role of the sibyl-queen is also different. There is no
trace here of the harlot-prophetess who appears in the
Greek, Slavonic and English versions. It would seem that
the redactor of the *Historia,* or his source, finding the
harlot-sibyl's sitting on the holy wood unseemly, rejected
this episode. Again we have to admit the possibility of influence from other sources. In the *Historia* it is only the
Queen's prophesying which links her to the sibyl. Here the
visit of the Queen to Solomon has the solemnity which it

has in III Kings 10. But the role of the Queen of Sheba who came and honored the wise King Solomon has been altered. Greek traditions of the prophesying sibyl, adapted to Christian purposes, had produced a sibyl-queen who was wiser than Solomon himself. Solomon, as representive of the Jewish kingdom, played a role second in importance to that of the gifted queen who, from a glance at the wood, prophesied its use in the Crucifixion. It would also seem that the New Testament has contributed to the change. In Matthew 12:42 (cf. Luke 11:31) we read that the Queen of the South (as she is called in the *Historia*) "shall rise in judgement with this generation, and shall condemn it: because she came from the ends of the earth to hear the wisdom of Solomon and behold a greater than Solomon is here." The queen who comes to Solomon in the *Historia* honors the wood, not the king; she comes to judge and condemn the kingdom which he represents. The episode of the Queen's visit has gained in dignity by being more closely related to Old Testament and, more important, New Testament sources. There is one other possible influence upon the changing character of the sibyl-queen: the traditional medieval interpretation of the Queen of Sheba's coming to Solomon as a prefiguration of the Magi honoring the Christ child, as a symbol of the pagan world adopting Christianity.[44] The sibyl-queen then represents the pagans who recognized the truth of Christianity more readily than did Solomon as a representative of the Jews.

We also observed in the Bodleian version that Solomon is not so much a precursor of Christ as a representative of the Jewish kingdom. Here in the *Historia* his role as Jewish king is even clearer: after hearing the prophecy concerning the wood, he expresses his hostility by having the tree stripped of the gold and hurled into a fishpond.[45]

The casting of the wood into the fishpond, where an angel descending to search for it stirred the water and brought about healings, is a new element—one which warrants some comment. It is evidently based on the following passage in John 5:2-4:

Now there is at Jerusalem a pond, called Probatica, which in Hebrew is named Bethsaida, having five porches. In these lay a great multitude of sick, of blind, of lame, of withered; waiting for the moving of the water. And an angel of the Lord descended at certain times into the pool; and the water was moved. And he that went down first into the pond after the motion of the water, was made whole.

The composer of the *Historia,* or his source, wishing to show Solomon's displeasure and to illustrate the holy quality of the wood, struck upon the idea that if the tree were thrown into the pond, the angel who moved the water might be looking for the wood. Thus the traditionally miraculous power of the pond was linked to the wood of the cross, and the rood-tree legend was provided with an episode which was to reappear in many succeeding versions.[46] Although this episode is entirely new to the legend, it bears this obvious resemblance to elements in the Bodleian version: the power of the wood to affect the quality of water and to heal. The addition of this episode reflects again the tendency of the author to use New Testament as well as Old Testament material.

The sixth element, the use of this wood to build the cross upon which Christ was crucified, is the point toward which the whole narrative has been moving. Unlike the Bodleian, to which the Helena legend has been joined, but like most other versions, the *Historia* ends with the Crucifixion.[47]

The Bodleian version and the *Historia,* though different in some respects, resemble each other in this: both extend the account of the wood back to an Old Testament figure—David or Moses. We shall consider next two other early forms of the rood-tree legend which extend the history of the wood back to an even earlier period.

In the morning the rods have taken root and have become one tree

Chapter 4

THE TWIGS
AND
THE SEED

The holy wood will fit nowhere

E XPLORATION into the origins of the rood-tree legend has thus far involved an analysis of the Bodleian version and the Latin *Historia,* the two earliest extant forms of the legend in the West. The Bodleian seems ultimately to have been derived from Eastern sources; the *Historia* is apparently related to both the Eastern and English versions.

Among the remaining rood-tree legends which lack the account of Seth's journey are two of special interest: one appears in Geoffrey of Viterbo's *Pantheon* (*ca.* 1180)[1] and the other was interpolated into Honorius of Autun's *De imagine mundi* between 1154 and 1159.[2] Both contain evidence of Eastern inflence and are, therefore, of some relevance to the problem of origin. But they are of greater importance in tracing the evolution of the legend since both extend the history of the wood to a time before Moses. Eventually, the legend included Adam and Seth, but in the *Pantheon* of Geoffrey of Viterbo an intermediate stage has been reached. Geoffrey's version brings the legend back to the time of the Flood and introduces a new character, Jonitus (Hiontus, Ionicus), who we are told is a son of Noah. He is carried to Paradise in a trance and returns with three twigs—fir, palm, and cypress.[3] He plants them in different places, but they come together and grow into one tree. This latter detail, it will be remembered, occurred in the Bodleian version in connection with Moses. Then, as in the Latin and English versions, David finds in the tree bearing three kinds of leaves a sign of the Trinity. The next episode we observed in the English and Slavonic versions: Solomon attempts to use the tree in building the Temple, but, however it is cut, it is always too long or too short. The rest of the story is similar to the *Historia*, except that the Queen of the South is also called Nicaula Sibylla. The *Pantheon* is then a composite version: its chief importance lies in its striking new beginning, the translation of Jonitus to Paradise.

Geoffrey referred to Athanasius as his source for the Jonitus episode, but the extant works of Athanasius contain no mention of this apocryphal son of Noah.[4] He appears, however, in the prophecies formerly attributed to Methodius,[5] but now assigned to an unknown author whom Ernst Sackur designated as Pseudo-Methodius.[6] The prophecies are extant only in Latin translations of a Greek text, which was itself, according to Marbury Ogle, "a reworking of a Syrian original."[7] Jonitus is then a figure who belonged specifically to Syriac tradition;[8] it was through his appearance in Pseudo-Methodius that he became known in the West. According to the Latin text, Jonitus was begotten one hundred years after the Flood.

The Quest of Seth

Noah later sent him to the land of the East, to the sea where the sun rises. He was given great wisdom by God and so became the discoverer of astronomy.[9] But there is no mention of his being translated to Paradise or of his returning with three twigs.

Meyer points out, what is fairly evident, that this apocryphal Jonitus probably developed from Enoch. We have already observed how the role of the apocryphal Enoch was extended to include Baruch and Moses and how the *Book of Enoch* influenced the earliest form of the Seth legend. The influence seems clearer in this episode of the rood-tree legend: the resemblance is seen in name (Enoch, Ionicus, Jonicus, Jonitus) and in function (both are transported to Paradise). Here the relationship ends and another tradition is responsible for Jonitus' taking back the three twigs. The *Pantheon* is only one of a long series of versions in which the tree of the cross is represented as having come from Paradise. It is clearly related to Jewish legends in which trees from Paradise—variously come by —are used for different holy purposes. There are Jewish traditions in which wood was taken from Paradise by Adam and was used as a rod by various Old Testament figures, including Moses; later it was used in the construction of the tabernacle.[10] In the Slavonic version of the rood-tree legend Eve and Seth, as well as Adam, take wood from Paradise, and in the Slavonic version of the *Vita* Eve and Seth take back three twigs of pine, cypress, and cedar.[11]

S. Baring-Gould suggests that Hiontus replaced Seth.[12] But, although complete evidence is not available, it is more likely that the opposite was the case. Geoffrey seems to be relating an early form of the legend in which the Seth and rood-tree legends had not been joined—at least in the West. It is doubtful whether once the two legends had been combined the pattern would be thus altered. As we we shall see, it is more probable that Seth replaced Hiontus.

As for Nicaula, the other new name in this version, we are dealing with a new line of influence, one which is of slight importance here but which in subsequent versions altered the form of the legend. Josephus relates that according to Herodotus, a queen ruled in Egypt whose name was Nikaulé; she was queen of Egypt and Ethiopia and went to visit King Solomon.[13] Here only the name indicates relationship. Other versions reveal that Ethiopian and related traditions of the Queen of the South contributed materially to the changing shape of the rood-tree legend.

There are additional differences between Geoffrey's and the earlier versions, but they are insignificant:[14] the main point of Geoffrey's account is that the wood for the cross came from three twigs which grew in Paradise.

Some significant changes in the legend appear in the interpolation which, according to Meyer, was made between 1154 and 1159 in Honorius of Autun's *De imagine mundi.*[15] A number of striking additions to the rood-tree legend are present, yet some of the episodes which we have previously considered are lacking. There is nothing of Jonitus or of his having been translated to Paradise. But there is the important extension of the narrative to include Adam. The idea that the wood of the cross came from Paradise is here, but it is expressed in an entirely different way. Instead of the three twigs which Jonitus brought back and planted, there is a kernel of the tree of knowledge which an angel placed in the mouth of Adam after his death.

There is nothing of Moses or David or of Solomon's attempt to use the wood in the construction of the Temple. Instead, the tree is still growing, as in the *Historia,* and Solomon is sitting under it when the sibyl-queen comes. The visit of the sibyl-queen is present in a more highly developed form than any we have yet encountered. That already complex figure has acquired goosefeet! Moreover, she does not give her prophecy orally, she writes it. New, too, and of importance in subsequent versions is the use of the wood as a bridge. But before attempting detailed comparisons we should consider this version more closely. Somewhat condensed, the legend is as follows:

[Honorius:] Adam was buried and rested for some time at Calvary, then was returned to Hebron, to the earth from which he had been taken. [Interpolation:] At the death of Adam an angel placed in his mouth a kernel from the tree of knowledge of good and evil. From this kernel grew a tree under which Solomon was sitting when he was visited by the Queen of Sheba. She was queen, not only of Sheba, but of Ethiopia; she was not only a queen, but a sibyl, and she had goosefeet and eyes bright as stars. When she saw the tree, she venerated it and ignored Solomon. Later Solomon's small half brother, who returned with her, asked her why she had venerated the tree and spurned the king. She wrote her answer to Solomon in the form of a prophecy. When he received it, he ordered that the tree be cut down, made into an altar and set in the Temple. At the time of the overthrow of Jerusalem by Nebuchadnezzar this altar was used as a bridge. Later it was thrown into a fishpond, which was visited daily by an angel, and, as a result, many sick people were cured. As the time of the Passion approached, the tree was taken from the water and of it the cross was made.

This account of the wood is almost totally different from the Bodleian and *Pantheon* versions. It resembles the *Historia,* which Meyer believes was one of the sources used by the interpolator, but more important are his other sources. Unlike the versions considered earlier, the *De imagine mundi* is not closely related to the Slavonic; it has been drawn from independent traditions.

Meyer refers to the composer as learned and imaginative.[16] Although his legend is admirable in certain respects, it finally impresses one as awkward and jumbled. The imperfections in structure, however, are characteristic of a legend still in the process of formation. As I hope to demonstrate, the roundabout, unmotivated, and incomplete actions are, in part, the result of the author's attempts to join diverging traditions. The legend at this stage of development, though lacking an effective form, is valuable as an illustration of tendencies and directions. Both the conflicting traditions and the general movements of the legend are apparent in the following new elements:

1. Adam is buried at Calvary, then carried back to Hebron.
2. An angel plants in Adam's mouth a kernel from the tree of knowledge of good and evil; the kernel grows into a tree.
3. The Queen of Sheba and Ethiopia has goosefeet; she writes her prophecy to Solomon.
4. Solomon has the tree cut down and made into an altar for the Temple.
5. The altar is used as a bridge.

The inclusion of Adam in the rood-tree legend was, of course, inevitable. In Christian theology the Crucifixion is believed to have been the consequence of the sin of Adam. As Saint Paul wrote, "By a man came death, and by a man the resurrection of the dead. And as in Adam all die, so in Christ all shall be made alive.[17] Irenaeus stated the case more explicitly: "By means of a tree we were made debtors to God, [so also] by means of a tree we may obtain remission of our debt."[18] The idea that Adam was buried on the site of the Crucifixion probably developed from this association of Adam and Christ, sin and salvation, and the two trees, the tree of knowledge symbolizing man's fall, and the tree of the cross, his redemption. The identification of the sites of Adam's burial and Christ's Crucifixion was facilitated by at least two additional factors. One was the meaning of the word Calvary or Golgotha (Latin *calvaria*, a "bare skull"; Hebrew *gulgōleth*, "skull"). The other was the existence of a Jewish tradition that Adam had been created in the center of the earth and buried in the same place, at Jerusalem, on the site of the Temple.[19] The tradition that Adam was buried at Calvary was then not entirely a Christian invention. It was rather a Christian adaptation of the Jewish legend. The center of the

Christian world was not the site of the Temple, but the site of the Crucifixion; hence the belief that it was at Calvary that Adam had been created and buried. According to F. Piper, Julius Africanus (ca. 221) was the first in the Christian church who identified Adam's grave as Golgotha.[20] Origen (third century) expresses the same view:

The body of the first man was buried there where Christ was crucified, so that "as in Adam all die, in Christ all are made alive," and in the place which is called Golgotha, i.e., the place of the skulls, the skull of the ancestor of men with all men received resurrection through the resurrection of our Saviour.[21]

Piper cites other early Fathers of the Greek Church who mention the tradition—Athanasius (295–373), Basil (ca. 330–79), John Chrysostom (347–407), and Epiphanius (ca. 315–402). As Piper states and as his citations bear out, the tradition that Adam's body lay at Golgotha or Calvary appeared often in the early Greek Fathers and became firmly established in the Greek Church.[22]

Just when the notion became known in the West is not certain, but Ambrose and Jerome[23] refer to it. In 386, Jerome wrote in a letter to Paula and Eustochium:

Tradition has it that in this city, nay, more, on this very spot, Adam lived and died. The place where our Lord was crucified is called Calvary, because the skull of primitive man was buried there.[24]

Although Jerome mentions the belief, he is opposed to it and points to another tradition of Adam's burial as more acceptable. This other tradition—also Jewish and probably the older of the two—represents Adam's burial place as Hebron.[25] According to Josue 14:15, "The name of Hebron before was called Cariath-Arbe: Adam the greatest among the Enacims was laid there." Hebron, of course, was the site of the family burial plot of Abraham.[26] The old name for Hebron, Cariath-Arbe, was interpreted to mean the city of the four and was believed to be the sepulcher not only of Abraham, Isaac, and Jacob, but also of the first man, Adam.[27]

Despite Jerome's attempt to re-establish the older belief that Adam was buried at Hebron, the view which prevailed in the Greek Church, that Adam was buried at Calvary, continued also to exist in the West.[28] It seems probable that Honorius knew of both traditions and was unable or unwilling to choose between them. The transference of Adam's body from Calvary back to Hebron may represent the author's attempt to reconcile two contradictory traditions.[29]

The next element is not an element in the true sense but a complex idea: a kernel, taken by an angel from the tree of knowledge and planted in Adam's mouth, grows into the tree which is used to form the cross. As far as I am aware, this idea appears in no earlier source. What we know of medieval legend-making, however, suggests that if this element were created by the author, it was created out of pre-existent material. Since the motif was to be very influential in the future evolution of the legend, we should consider some of the traditions which may have been used in its formation.

The first of these traditions, that Adam was buried by an angel, was prevalent in the pseudepigraphic literature of the Jews. In Ginzberg's reconstruction of the lost Hebrew Adambook the three great archangels bury him.[30] In *The Apocalypse of Moses,* in one text the burial is carried out by Michael and in other texts by Michael, Gabriel, Uriel, and Raphael;[31] in the *Vita Adae et Evae* it is Michael and Uriel who bury Adam.[32] In the Ethiopian *Book of Adam and Eve* he was buried after the Flood by an angel and Shem.[33]

This pseudepigraphic literature contains no mention of the angel's placing a kernel in Adam's mouth. But, there is an appropriateness about the motif: the mouth which was the source of sin becomes the source of salvation; as sin came into the world through the mouth, by Adam's eating the forbidden fruit, so salvation would come through a tree which grew from a kernel of the forbidden tree, placed in the sinner's mouth. This relationship between the means through which man sinned and the means through which he is saved is a very old one and can be found in various forms in Jewish apocryphal literature.[34] Among the early Christian writers who point out the connection between the tree of knowledge and the rood-tree are Irenaeus, Tertullian, Julius Firmicus Maternus, and Augustine.[35] However ancient and widespread was this concept of a relationship between the sources of sin and salvation, the first actual statement that the cross was made of the wood of the tree of knowledge is, according to Otto Zöckler, to be found in the Greek writer, Anastasius Sinaitica (*ca.* 650).[36]

The motif of the tree growing from the dead Adam is paralleled by the folk belief that a plant grows from the body of a buried person. This belief is present in the folk literature of many peoples, including the Persians, Greeks, Celts, Germans, and Slavs.[37] Sometimes a flower or tree is represented as growing from the mouth of the deceased, as in folk songs cited by A. Koberstein.[38] The living tree emerging from the dead body, an ancient and striking form of the belief in immortality, serves in the rood-tree legend as an effective prefiguration of the cross of Christ, erected upon the bones of Adam. In folklore, however, the tree stems from the soul of the dead person, not from a kernel. In our legend the kernel is a physical link connecting the tree of knowledge as the origin of death and the tree of the cross as the means to eternal life.

Another possible influence on the formation of this motif is the imagery of Isaiah. Might not Isaiah's phrase, "rod of his mouth,"[39] have suggested the tree in the mouth? Or his prophecy of the tree of Jesse, so widely represented in the glass and stone of the Middle Ages?[40] The tree is usually portrayed as rooted in the body of the outstretched Jesse, but there are instances of its growing from the mouth. The abbé Corblet notes a stained glass window at Saint Antoine's in Compiègne in which the trunk stems from the mouth.[41] And M. Didron observes, at Reims, in a *Bible historiale,* the tree rising from the mouth of Jesse. As he remarks, "Il s'agit donc là, d'une génération intellectuelle plutôt que charnelle. C'est la tête, c'est la parole, c'est la pensée, et non l'estomac ou les intestins, qui mettent au monde Marie et Jésus. Jésus, en effet, c'est le Verbe fait chair, c'est la parole divine."[42]

From whatever traditions it was derived, the image of the tree growing from Adam's mouth became a standard motif in the rood-tree legend. It was at once a symbol of immortality and a prefiguration of the cross arising from Adam's grave on Golgotha.

Neither is the next "element" simple; the queen who visits Solomon is Sheba, an Ethiopian and a sibyl as well as a queen; she has goosefeet and eyes bright as stars. She does not speak to Solomon concerning the tree but writes to him. We have seen earlier that the Queen of Sheba was fused with the sibyl, Sabbe. In the Bodleian version she was more the sibyl; in the *Historia* she was more clearly the Queen of Sheba. In Geoffrey's version she was Nicaula, Queen of Egypt and Ethiopia. In the interpolated *De imagine mundi* the most striking new feature which has been attached to the sibyl-queen is goosefeet.

Although the queen with goosefeet is a stranger to the rood-tree legend, she was a familiar figure in French ecclesiastical architecture of the twelfth century, appearing at Toulouse, Dijon, Nesle, Nevers, and Saint-Pourçain. Jacob Grimm traced this figure of the queen with goosefeet, known as *reine pédauque,* to the swan-maiden and the splay-footed spinning woman of German mythology, Berhte.[43] Karl Simrock, who similarly associated *reine pédauque* with Berhte, further identified the figures of her on French cathedrals as the Queen of Sheba.[44] The spindle which she holds at Toulouse would seem to confirm the views of Grimm and Simrock that the form of this statue and probably the others was influenced by German myths, especially those of Berhte. A fusion evidently occurred between the prophesying Queen of Sheba and Berhte, the spinning woman who knew the future because she spun the web of fate.[45] An additional detail in our version tends to confirm the theory that the Queen of Sheba and Berhte were fused: the Queen has eyes as bright as stars, and Berhte in Old High German is Perahta (the bright, luminous, glorious).[46] The actual goosefeet may well have come from the earlier fusion of the prophesying swan-maiden and the spinner, Berhte.[47] Our author might then have drawn upon the plastic art of the period for the detail of the Queen's goosefeet. Or he might have drawn upon these more ancient Teutonic myths. For the detail that the Queen's eyes were bright as stars he more probably was indebted to literary sources. In either case, Germanic influence would thus far seem likely.

Moses Gaster, however, believes that the origin of the Queen's goosefeet is to be found in oriental tradition. At first his theory seems unnecessarily farfetched, but on closer analysis one discovers that it accounts for an otherwise inexplicable detail in the *De imagine mundi:* the use of the wood as a bridge. According to Gaster, ancient oriental traditions attest to the dubious nature of the Queen of Sheba's feet. The Targum Sheni to the Book of Esther, which Gaster placed at latest in the second half of the seventh century, contains the following passage:

When King Solomon heard that the Queen of Saba had come, he sat in a glass house. The Queen, who meanwhile had come nearer, saw him sitting inside, and thinking that he sat in a pool, tied up her clothes, to wade through the water. Solomon now saw that she had hair on her feet.[48]

This legend, probably Jewish in origin, was related frequently in Arabic literature; it appears in a similar, though even more abbreviated, form in the Koran.[49] The oldest detailed version is found in the Arabic world chronicle of Tabari (Thâlabî), dated tenth century by Wilhelm Hertz, eleventh by Anton Berlinger.[50] Here the Queen of Sheba is called Bilkis, and we are told that she has ass's feet. The reason given for this peculiarity is that though her father was a prince, her mother was a demon.[51] An explanation is also supplied for Solomon's building the glass house or glass floor with water beneath: he had been forewarned of Bilkis' demon origin and hoped, by this contrivance, to trick her into revealing the evidence of her descent.[52] It would seem that the accounts in the Targum Sheni and Koran, which mention only the hair, represent faded versions of more primitive stories in which the Queen had real ass's feet.[53] There are, however, a number of problems connected with accepting this theory of the oriental origin of the Queen's goosefeet.

1. In the oriental traditions the Queen has goat's or ass's feet— in Western versions, goosefeet.
2. Only the goosefeet appear in our legend; nothing else of the episode.
3. There is the problem of transmission.

We might consider first how the ass's feet became goosefeet. As Hertz observed, it is very probable that a copyist read instead of "pedes asininos," "pedes anserinos." This shift may have been an unconscious error or a deliberate change. Hertz considers the latter case likely, especially in view of the legends of the prophesying swan-maiden which would have been familiar to a German copyist.[54] Whether by unconscious error or deliberate change, the Queen of Sheba was given goosefeet, not ass's feet. For whatever reason the change was made, it was a fitting one; the queen who prophesied concerning the Messiah was more appropriately related to the divine swan-maiden than to the demon Bilkis.

One wonders why, however, if our author were acquainted with the whole episode contained in the oriental versions, he would mention only the goosefeet. One possibility is that he found the narrative related so briefly as to be unintelligible and so omitted the episode and retained only the odd detail. This possibility becomes more likely when we consider the use of the wood as a bridge. As we mentioned earlier, the goosefeet and the "eyes bright as stars" might have been drawn from French and German sources. It is for an explanation of the use of the wood as a bridge that we turn to oriental tradition. The bridge itself does not appear in any of the Jewish or Arabic versions we have considered; it first appeared when the oriental story was adapted to fit the rood-tree legend.[55]

We have seen in the *De imagine mundi* that when the Queen arrives, the wood is not in the Temple; it is a growing tree, and Solomon is sitting under it. After the Queen's visit the tree is placed in the Temple, and later still it is used as a bridge. In subsequent versions, which illustrate more clearly the influence of oriental traditions, the wood is being used as a bridge when the Queen arrives. In these later accounts the whole episode has been very effectively adapted to fit the rood-tree legend: when the Queen appears, the wood is being used as a bridge (because of Solomon's displeasure with its stretching and shrinking powers). The Queen, who has goosefeet, recognizing the holy nature of the wood, refuses to step on it, but instead lifts up her skirts and wades through the stream. The goosefeet are then transformed into human feet, and the Queen delivers her prophecy.[56] This form of the episode, which clearly resembles the oriental versions, appears in many rood-tree legends from Johannes Beleth on.

It is our problem to determine, if we can, whether the author had such a Christianized form of the story before him. Again it would be difficult to see why, if the author knew the whole episode, he would alter it so unsuccessfully. On the other hand, if he did not know this version, how are we to account for his introducing the bridge? Could it be that oral transmission might account in some way for the abbreviated and jumbled form of the episode? Or could there have been deliberate changes—omissions and rearrangement of material to suit a particular purpose? There is one point which might explain the reordering of these elements. We have seen in earlier versions that Solomon in his rejection of the prophecy concerning the wood represents the Jews who later rejected Christ himself. In the *De imagine mundi,* however, after the prophecy Solomon shows veneration for the wood by placing it in the Temple; here his role as ancestor of Christ is stressed. It is barely possible that it was to emphasize Solomon's prefigurative relationship to Christ[57] that the author rearranged his material: Solomon placed the tree in the Temple after the prophecy and not before. It was not he who ordered the inappropriate use of the wood as a bridge; this occurrence was assigned to the period following the overthrow of Jerusalem.

We might look next at the problem of transmission. Hertz concludes that the way in which the oriental legend was transmitted to the West remains a mystery.[58] According to Berlinger, the story went to Spain, then to France where it acquired the goosefeet, and in this form went to Germany.[59] Gaster notes that the story, in its transmission from the Orient to the Occident, seems to have left traces in the Sicilian legend of Magus Heliodor. This version appears in the *Acta sanctorum:*

Alias (mulieres) iter facientes, falsa fluminis specie objecta, indecore nudari compulit, et per siccum pulveram, quasi aquam inambulare.[60]

It must be admitted that the case for oriental influence on this particular element is far from clear.

We turn to one final point in our analysis of the Queen in the *De imagine mundi* version: she does not deliver her prophecy to Solomon orally; she writes it. Two main traditions seem to have converged to produce the written prophecy. First, the Jewish and Arabic sources which we have been considering mention a correspondence between

Solomon and the Queen. In the account given in the Targum Sheni, Solomon sends a letter to the Queen and she sends a reply; similarly in the Koran.[61] Second, in the rood-tree legend itself we noted the tradition of attributing Sibylline Oracles to the Queen of Sheba. In the *Historia* the Queen delivers a prophecy from the Sixth Book; in the *De imagine mundi* the Queen's prophecy comes from the Eighth or Acrostic Book. This prophecy is included in *The Oration of Constantine*, and in Augustine's *City of God*,[62] where it is attributed to the Erythraean sibyl. The initial Greek letter of each of twenty-seven lines spells out the Greek words for "Jesus Christ the Son of God, the Savior." The prophecy itself, however, concerns Christ's coming at the Last Judgment, not Christ's death on the cross. I quote the first five lines in English translation:

Judgement shall moisten the earth with the sweat of its standard,
Ever enduring, behold the King shall come through the ages,
Sent to be here in the flesh, and judge at the last of the world.
O God, the believing and the faithless alike shall behold Thee
Uplifted with saints, when last the ages are ended.[63]

There also appears in connection with this prophecy a new figure, the small brother of Solomon. But since he is not important in the evolving rood-tree legend, we can do little here but refer the reader to other sources.[64]

We have then in this version five new elements. The first two concern the inclusion of Adam in the story: his burial at Calvary and Hebron and the angel's planting in his mouth a kernel from the tree of knowledge. This idea that the wood of the cross came from Paradise is also present in Geoffrey's version, but in a different form. In the *Pantheon* three twigs—fir, palm, and cypress—were taken from Paradise by Jonitus and planted. In the *De imagine mundi* a kernel, not a twig, is taken from Paradise; it is a kernel of the tree of knowledge, and it is planted in the mouth of Adam. The appearance of the kernel is a very significant innovation and one which was exceedingly popular in subsequent versions. From this introduction of the kernel developed a new form of the rood-tree legend; henceforth there were the twig and the kernel versions.

The remaining three elements of the *De imagine mundi* involve Solomon and the Queen of Sheba. The episode of the Queen's visit and prophecy, though present in all other versions, appears here with significant variants. Chief among these are the goosefeet and the written prophecy, both of which seem to indicate oriental influence. The use of the wood in the Temple is not a new element, but it has been placed in a different position: after the prophecy rather than before. As we suggested, the rearrangement of the material may have been intended to enhance Solomon's prefigurative relationship to Christ. The use of the wood as a bridge is new. Although in this version the bridge is dissociated from the Queen's visit, it probably comes from oriental traditions in which the bridge and the Queen are closely connected, as they are in all other versions.

The final episode is one which we have met before—the wood was thrown into a fishpond and there caused healings. The existence of this episode helps to establish the fact that the *De imagine mundi* version is related to the other forms of the legend. In precisely what way, it is difficult to determine at this point. The problem may be further clarified by our study of the way in which the rood-tree and Seth legends were joined.

St. Maximilla sitting on the wood, her clothes catch alight

Chapter 5

SETH AND THE TWIG
FROM
PARADISE

The wood used as a footbridge over a brook

THE ROOD-TREE legends which were not connected with the Seth story vary considerably in structure and extent. Some, beginning with Moses or David, seem to have been cut off from their sources and, as in the case of the Bodleian version, to have been combined with another legend (that of Saint Helena). Others—like the interpolation in the *De imagine mundi*—seem complete, beginning with the death of Adam and ending with the Crucifixion.

Of the same extent as the latter and appearing at approximately the same time are versions in which the Seth and rood-tree legends form a continuous narrative. How were these versions formed? Did they develop from a joining of two originally independent stories or did the rood-tree legend evolve from the Seth legend?

The main point of the Seth–rood-tree legend is the same as that of the *De imagine mundi* version: the wood of the cross came from Paradise and grew on Adam's grave. But this idea is presented differently in the early forms of the legend: it is not an angel who places a kernel of the tree of knowledge in Adam's mouth; it is Seth who gets a branch of the tree and plants it on Adam's grave. At this point the Seth–rood-tree legend resembles rather closely Geoffrey's version in which Jonitus was translated to Paradise and returned with three twigs. Leaving these relationships for the moment, we shall first examine in detail an early form of the legend of Seth and the holy cross.

Meyer cites the *Rationale divinorum officiorum* of Johannes Beleth (*ca.* 1170) as the oldest source for Seth's going to Paradise and returning with a twig which became the cross.[1] Seth's getting a twig was also interpolated into four twelfth-century manuscripts of the *Vita Adae et Evae* (thus forming what Meyer calls the Class III manuscripts). Although there is no available evidence to prove these interpolations to have been earlier than 1170, they represent the legend at an earlier point in its evolution and will, therefore, be considered first.

It will be recalled that in the original *Vita* the Seth legend consists of Adam's sending Eve and Seth to Paradise to get the oil of mercy. The earliest Christian adaptation of the legend includes the prophecy that Christ will bring the oil. In the Class III manuscripts of the *Vita,* the legend has been further Christianized by the interpolation of material which connects Seth's journey with the wood of the cross. This new material is introduced at the point at which Eve and Seth are leaving Paradise:[2] the angel took from the tree of knowledge a twig with three leaves and gave it to Seth. But as Seth was crossing the Jordan, the twig fell into the water. Seth reported to his father what had happened; Adam bade him return and get the twig

The Quest of Seth

from the river. When Seth brought the twig back, Adam rejoiced and commanded his son to plant it at the head of his grave. Seth did as he was told, and after Adam's death the twig grew to be a mighty tree. Later Solomon's hunters found the tree. They adorned it and placed it in the Temple. When the Queen of Sheba saw the tree, she prophesied that one would die on it who would destroy the kingdom of the Jews. The tree was then thrown into the *probatica piscina* where it effected cures. At the time of the Crucifixion, the tree was used to form the cross.[3]

The rood-tree legend which has been interpolated into the *Vita* is a simple one: the only elements not met previously are those which relate to Seth, which join Seth's journey to the legend of the cross. These new elements will be explored presently, but of more immediate interest is the relationship between the two stories.

It is apparent at once that the rood-tree material is extraneous to the Seth story. The following instances will make this point clear:

1. Eve and Seth are refused the oil of mercy; they are told that Christ will be the oil of mercy; they are given the twig. Here is an accretion of motifs representing three stages of development: the original *Vita*, the Christian adaptation, and the inclusion of material from a third source, which we shall discuss presently.
2. The archangel Michael, who delivers the prophecy, is later referred to as "the angel."
3. There is the curious behavior of Seth: he dropped the twig in the Jordan, continued home, then returned to get it.
4. In the section in which the twig is introduced, there is no mention of Eve.

Each of these points suggests that material has been added but not assimilated. Although unsatisfactory as narrative, the interpolated *Vita* provides a valuable text for a study of the legend-making process. First, there are the new elements:

1. An angel takes from the tree of knowledge a twig with three leaves and gives it to Seth.
2. The twig falls into the Jordan and is later retrieved by Seth.
3. The twig is planted on Adam's grave and becomes a tree.

The first element, that an angel gave Seth a branch from the tree of knowledge, suggests the interesting possibility that we may be dealing with an earlier form of the Seth legend than the one in *The Apocalypse of Moses*. There are shreds of evidence from many quarters to suggest that there existed earlier forms of the Seth legend in which Seth went to Paradise and returned with a twig, probably from the tree of life. We shall consider one by one these pieces of evidence. Taken together, they point to the existence in Hebrew of an ancient Seth story, translated into Greek, there probably combined with the story of Seth's journey for the oil, Christianized first by the inclusion of the Messianic prophecy and later by the addition of rood-tree material, and finally translated into Slavonic, Armenian, and Latin.

Since it is our thesis that in the earliest form of the Seth legend the object sought was the twig, not the oil, we should consider the role of the twig in ancient myth and ritual. Both the twig and oil played an important part in primitive rites and for the same underlying reason. Both were believed to be embodiments of the life spirit which dwelt in the tree from which they were taken.[4] But whereas it took a degree of civilization to enable man to extract oil from trees,[5] the plucking of a twig was an obvious and ready means of procuring the indwelling spirit. As a natural object, the twig was one of the earliest symbols and played a central part in rituals as diverse as fertility rites, rain ceremonies, healing rituals,[6] and ceremonies of enthronement.[7] Mrs. van Buren in her study of Mesopotamian iconography referred to a number of ancient Near Eastern artifacts which depict a plant or branch with three leaves.[8] The plant is frequently held by a figure who

in some representations has been identified as Gilgamesh.[9]
We considered earlier the possible relationship between
Seth's journey for the oil and Gilgamesh's quest for eternal
life. Here the stories resemble one another more closely:
both heroes get a branch or plant which represents immortality.

There is a magic plant known to the ancient Greeks as
moly, which Hermes gives to Odysseus.[10] According to
Goblet d'Alviella, Hermes' plant was a three-leaved branch
and the original form of the caduceus.[11] There is also in
Greek mythology the willow branch which enables Or-
pheus to penetrate the lower world.[12]

The twig or plant, then, is frequently represented in the
ancient traditions of the peoples who concern us most:
the Babylonians, the Jews, and the Greeks.[13] Originally
connected with fertility rites, the bough was also used in
rain-making ceremonies, in healing rituals, and in ceremonies surrounding the enthronement of the divine king.
As a magic talisman, it enabled the hero to enter the other
world; as a symbol of immortality, it was the object of the
quest of Gilgamesh.

Having considered—though briefly—the use of the twig
in ancient ritual, myth, and story, we should return to a
motif which was discussed in connection with *The Apocalypse of Moses*, the journey to the Earthly Paradise. We
referred there to the pattern common in Jewish apocrypha
of an Old Testament character translated to Paradise.
Enoch seems to have been the original, with the translation of Moses, Baruch, and others modeled upon his. The
apocryphal Seth was also based to some extent on Enoch.
But the difference mentioned earlier should be stressed
here—the difference between the journey and the translation, between the Earthly Paradise and the Heavenly
Paradise. *The Apocalypse of Moses* and *The Book of
Enoch*, produced in a similar milieu, resemble each other
in some respects, but the differences are marked and can
best be accounted for by admitting that *The Apocalypse*

represents the kernel of an older tale. The conception of Paradise as a place to which Seth could walk originated in a more primitive time than the conception of the Heavenly Paradise to which Enoch had to be transported. The translation of Seth mentioned by Georgius Syncellus and Georgius Cedrenus may well represent a transferring to Seth of the former role of Enoch.[14] This transference was very likely made because Seth was already a full-fledged hero. Seth in his journey to the Earthly Paradise is the more ancient hero; his story probably antedates the account of the ascent of Enoch into the elaborate Heavenly Paradise of apocalyptic literature. A very interesting form of the combined legends represents Seth, translated to Paradise, returning with a twig.[15] Here Seth's journey appears as a translation to the Heavenly Paradise to correspond with the interests of a later time. In this account the Seth–rood-tree legend most closely resembles the Jonitus version. Both seem to have been influenced by the apocryphal Enoch and his translation to the Heavenly Paradise.

Having considered the antiquity of the twig as a ritual object and the Earthly Paradise as a more primitive concept than the Heavenly and Seth as the more ancient hero than Enoch, we should proceed to examine various Jewish legends in which a branch was taken from Paradise. According to some of these legends, when Adam and Eve were driven from the Garden of Eden, they took a branch, which later became the staff of Moses.[16] There are other accounts which relate that Moses himself went to Paradise and cut his staff from the tree of life.[17] The latter accounts resemble the Seth legend more closely in that an Old Testament figure gains access to Paradise and returns with wood. There is another legend preserved in Hebrew in the *Gali Razia, The Revealed Secrets,* a Kabalistic work, according to Gershom Scholem, written in 1552 by an anonymous author.[18] Here it is related that Adam sent Seth to Paradise to ask God's mercy. The angels gave Seth a branch, plucked from the tree of life, and told him to plant it so that when it produced its first fruits, the mercy of God would descend into them and the gates of Heaven would be open. Seth took the branch and planted it in the desert; later Moses found it and from it cut his rod.

There is discernible behind these ancient stories, especially those in which Adam or Seth returns from Paradise with a branch, the desire of man to possess a relic from the Garden of Eden, where he formerly lived in harmony with God.[19] In the stories in which Moses got the wood, a related idea has been added: miracles, such as those Moses performed with his rod, represent a renewal of this harmony and they take place by means of an object brought from Paradise.

Although a late work, the *Gali Razia* may have preserved an ancient tradition. In any case, the Seth story it relates clearly resembles the two preceding legends in which the rod of Moses came from Paradise. It would seem that this legend was translated from Hebrew into Greek (like *The Apocalypse of Moses*), though no Greek form is extant. We do, however, have Slavonic and Armenian versions, based on the Greek, which represent essentially the same story, except that it has been Christianized; the branch becomes, not the rod of Moses, but the wood of the cross.

Presumably the Jewish legend that Seth brought a branch from Paradise is based on the older stories that it was Adam and Eve or Moses who brought the wood. Ginzberg has provided the clue, I think, to the transference of the story to Seth. As he pointed out, the name Seth has been interpreted to mean plant, and the legend concerning Seth and the branch of the tree of life may be related to this interpretation of his name.[20] A passage preserved in an Armenian text strongly supports this association of the branch and the name Seth. In the first part of "The History of the Repentance of Adam and Eve," Adam is given a branch by the angel Gabriel as a sign that a son shall be born to them whom they shall call Seth.[21]

Seth and the Twig from Paradise   93

Before leaving the *Gali Razia* version we might note an interesting difference between it and the stories in which Adam or Moses takes the branch: the angels give the branch to Seth; he does not take it. This may seem to be a minor point, but the Adam and Moses stories correspond to the archetype which C. G. Jung mentions of the hero who takes the sacred object, the herb of immortality or the golden bough.[22] The angels who give Seth the twig in the *Gali Razia*—and in all other versions of the Seth legend—represent a later stage of development: the angels are intermediaries between man and God, and their giving the branch is a token of renewed harmony between man and his Creator, against whom he had transgressed. The giving of the branch represents man's recognition that the sacred object cannot be seized; it must be given.

In the Hebrew version the branch comes, not from the tree of knowledge, as in most Christianized versions, but from the tree of life. Although not present in the original account of Genesis (the J^1 document), the tree of life was an exceedingly ancient concept and was introduced into the second stratum (J^2).[23] It is mentioned along with the tree of knowledge in Genesis 2:9 and again in 3:22–24: after Adam had eaten the forbidden fruit, he was driven from Paradise "lest perhaps he put forth his hand, and take also of the tree of life, and eat, and live forever." "Before the paradise of pleasure were placed Cherubims [*sic*], and a flaming sword, turning every way, to keep the way of the tree of life." Here then in the tree of life, growing in the Terrestrial Paradise, was the gift of immortality, withheld, yet tantalizing the imagination with its accessibility. In apocalyptic literature its fruit supplied eternal life to the righteous in the hereafter; in legends its wood provided the substance for the marvelous rod of Moses.

If the story of Seth and the branch in the *Gali Razia* represents an authentic ancient Jewish tradition, then we have an exceedingly valuable document, the only extant Hebrew version of Seth's journey to Paradise. It must therefore figure largely in our consideration of the earliest form of the Seth legend. Here Seth is given a branch; there is no mention of oil. The phrase, "oil of mercy," as we noted in chapter 1, was probably not in the original Hebrew, but was coined in Greek. Once the term was created, it became enormously popular in Greek and later in Latin. In the centuries immediately preceding and following the Christian era and in succeeding times oil was a more fitting symbol than the branch, which it replaced. But the branch, because it was so readily associated with the wood of the cross, was later reintroduced.

In Jewish apocryphal literature (extant in Greek) it is not oil but the tree of life which is promised to the faithful at the Resurrection.[24] In Greek—apart from the Jewish apocryphal works—there is little extant to provide evidence for the twig version's antedating the oil version, but what there is seems to support our theory. In the Greek version of *The Gospel of Nicodemus* the archangel Michael asks Seth if he wants the oil or the tree from which the oil comes. Might two levels be here preserved: the earlier in which Seth asks for a branch of the tree and the latter in which he asks for the oil?[25]

We should also look a little more closely at the Greek *Apocalypse of Moses* to see how, if possible, the rood-tree legend might have developed from it. This line of inquiry is based on the belief that there were versions of *The Apocalypse*, now lost, which corresponded to the *Vita*. As we noted earlier, one of the differences between *The Apocalypse* and the *Vita* is that whereas in the former Adam took the seeds from Paradise at the expulsion, in the latter Eve and Seth took them when they were refused the oil. Although the point is not essential to our thesis, it would seem that this shift in material, which appears in the *Vita* but not in the extant manuscripts of *The Apocalypse*, was present in the Greek version from which the Latin was derived. These Greek texts may have contained not only the substitution of Eve and Seth's taking the

Seth and the Twig from Paradise   95

herbs for Adam's taking them but also the interpolation of the Christian prophecy from *The Gospel of Nicodemus.* (The original *Gospel of Nicodemus* was in Greek.) Both innovations point toward the development of a rood-tree legend: *The Gospel* provided the Christianization, and Seth's taking the herbs may have led to the substitution of Seth's taking the branch, especially if there were already stories of Seth's bringing a branch to Adam.

More important evidence pointing to the existence in Greek of such a legend survives in Slavonic and Armenian, both derived from Greek. In Slavonic literature a number of traces of this connection between Seth and the twig have been preserved. In Old Church Slavonic, for instance, there is an Adambook, derived from Greek,[26] in which Seth's journey is related very much as it is in the *Vita.* But before Eve and Seth leave Paradise, Michael gives them three twigs of the tree of knowledge. Seth brings the twigs to Adam, who makes himself a wreath with them. He is buried with the wreath, which grows into a great tree.[27] Another Slavonic work, *The Confession of Eve,* also derived from Greek sources but resembling the Latin *Vita* more than the Greek *Apocalypse,* also tells of Seth's going to Paradise and getting a branch of the tree of knowledge.[28] The Slavonic rood-tree legend, which we referred to earlier, includes in the account of the third—or God's—tree, a narrative that may represent the old form of the Seth legend. Seth brought Adam a branch of a tree from Paradise. With the branch Adam made a wreath and with it he was buried. From the wreath grew a great tree (which was ultimately used to form the cross).[29] The fact that the wreath appears in the Slavonic and not in the Latin version may mean either that it was a Slavonic addition or that the Western form of the legend was based on a variant Greek text in which the wreath was not mentioned.

According to Vatroslav Jagić, the Slavonic Adambook in which Michael gives Eve and Seth the three branches is

The Quest of Seth

the origin of the rood-tree legend.[30] According to Gaster, it is in Slavonic that the oldest and most complete version of the combined Seth and rood-tree legend has been preserved.[31]

There are Armenian, as well as Slavonic, Adam legends derived from the Greek.[32] Jacques Issaverdens and Erwin Preuschen have each translated a number of these Adam-books: the former, into English; the latter, into German. Among the most relevant to our purpose is the one entitled "The History of the Repentance of Adam and Eve," to which we referred previously. Here Eve and Seth go to Paradise for "a branch of the tree that yields oil."[33] Here we may have preserved the two strata, the branch and the oil. In a fragment entitled "Adam's Words unto Seth," an angel gives Seth "a branch of joy," which Seth gives to his father. Adam places it on his eyes and they are opened. He sees it is a branch of the tree of knowledge.[34]

As Adolf Jacoby concludes, "Der Zweig ist an die Stelle des Öles der Barmherzigkeit in der ältesten Tradition getreten."[35] Originally Jewish, these versions of Seth and the branch were probably—like the Jewish Adambook—translated into Greek, although the Greek versions are not extant. At some point—perhaps in Greek—the story of Seth and the branch was combined with the story of Seth's journey for the oil of mercy. It was probably in Greek, too, that the rood-tree legend developed. The combined Seth and rood-tree legend seems then to have been translated from Greek into Slavonic, Armenian, and Latin. Thus far one would say it was probably from the Greek that the Class III manuscripts of the *Vita* were derived.

A consideration of the second element—Seth's dropping the twig into the Jordan and being sent back by Adam to get it—may alter our assumption. This is the sort of detail which, from a narrative point of view, is awkward and meaningless. It has, however, symbolic meaning, especially when considered in relation to earlier traditions. There is nothing which corresponds to it in either the Slavonic or Armenian Adambooks, but in the Slavonic rood-tree legend there is a similar episode. It is related there that the first of the three trees—Adam's tree—fell into the Tigris at the time of the Fall of Adam and Eve and was later taken out.[36] Here the falling twig clearly represents the Fall of Man.

Seth's dropping the twig into the water gains an even richer symbolical value when compared to the somewhat similar episode in *The Epic of Gilgamesh*. It will be recalled that Gilgamesh got his plant of immortality from the water. This link between Gilgamesh and Seth is more firmly established by the fact that the plant of Gilgamesh, as well as the branch of Seth, is represented with three leaves. But as the Gilgamesh story is one of immortality, found and lost, the Seth story is one of immortality, given, lost, and regained. Our tale relates not only the fall but the redemption. Seth's twig, which is lost, is also recovered and thus becomes a symbol for man's own fall and restoration. For the twig became in the fulness of time the wood of the cross, the instrument of man's salvation. This twig then is the link between the wood which caused man's fall and the wood which made possible his redemption.

The immersion of the twig acquires a further dimension in terms of the ancient relationship between the tree of life and the water of life. Widengren stresses the relationship between the two in the myths and rituals of the ancient Mesopotamians.[37] Especially interesting is the ritual dipping of the twig in the water. According to Frazer, a number of peoples, including ancient Greeks, Romans, and Russians, performed a ritual which consisted of dipping the branch into water and sprinkling the moisture.[38] Originally to assure fertility of the soil, the ritual was also performed in Babylonia and Assyria to cure the sick.[39] In each case it seems to have been a purificatory rite intended to banish the evil spirits which bring blight to crops, animals, and men. It will be remembered also that Aeneas, as he stands at the gateway of the lower world, sprinkles water, probably with the golden bough.[40]

As the immersion of the twig in water suggests ancient purificatory rites, so does it suggest the Christian rite of baptism. From the regenerative waters of the Jordan the tree of knowledge comes forth cleansed of its association with man's fall and ready to serve in the great redemptive act of the Crucifixion.

The third element, that Seth planted the branch on Adam's grave, needs little comment. It is paralleled by the motif of the tree growing on the grave of the deceased which appeared in the *De imagine mundi* version. The remaining elements of the Class III manuscripts of the *Vita* we have met before; they correspond very closely to those in the *Historia*.

We might, therefore, account for the interpolated *Vita* in somewhat the following way: the Latin version of Seth's journey for the oil was a popular work in western Europe in the tenth, eleventh, and twelfth centuries; from the East, through exactly what channels we cannot say— whether directly from the Greek or with a Slavonic intermediary—came the story of Seth's getting a twig from Paradise. The two stories were probably already combined so that Seth journeyed for oil, but returned with a twig, which was eventually used to form the cross.

A slightly different form of the combined Seth and rood-tree legends appears in the *Rationale divinorum officiorum* of Johannes Beleth, which Meyer dated after 1170.[41] The first part—the Seth legend—is a shortened form of the Class III manuscripts of the *Vita*: Adam sends Seth to Paradise; Seth returns with a branch which he plants on Adam's grave. Then, as in the Bodleian version, attempts to use the tree in building Solomon's Temple are futile. The next section is exceedingly important: though briefly related, it contains the earliest extant form of the episode of which we spoke in connection with the *De imagine mundi* version—the placing of the wood over a ditch, the coming of the Queen of Sheba, her adoration of the wood, and her refusal to step on it. The final episodes have been met before: the wood is thrown into the *probatica piscina* and is used to make the cross.

We shall consider only one other version in which the Seth and rood-tree legends have been joined. The text of this version, which Meyer designated IV 6, was put together from various manuscripts.[42] The first part resembles the interpolated *Vita:* the angel gave Eve and Seth a branch (with three leaves) from the tree of knowledge; Seth dropped the branch in the Jordan and Adam sent him back to get it; Seth planted it on Adam's grave; the tree was adorned by Solomon and placed in the Temple; the Queen of Sheba prophesied; the wood was hurled into the *probatica piscina;* it was used for the cross. This version would not be mentioned here were it not for one detail which appears at the end: the trunk of this wood was placed on Calvary where Adam was buried so that the blood of the Savior would fall on the head of the first-formed. This motif is related to one which we discussed in connection with the *De imagine mundi* version: Adam was buried on the site of the Crucifixion. The additional detail that Christ's blood dropped upon the skull of Adam and restored him to life also existed from early times and was probably based on the literal interpretation of the passage in Ephesians 5:14: "Awake, thou that sleepest and arise from the dead and Christ shall give thee light" (cf. Matt. 27:52–53). The idea appears in a metrical work attributed to Tertullian, in Epiphanius, and in Jerome.[43] According to Jerome, Adam was not restored to life, but his sins were washed away. Gaster mentions the occurrence of the idea in tenth-century Slavonic literature.[44] Early twelfth-century visitors to the Holy Land, Saewulf and Abbot Daniel, reported that the belief was still current there.[45] As for the rood-tree legend, although a number of versions relate that the Crucifixion took place on the site

The Quest of Seth

of Adam's grave, few mentioned this detail of Adam's literal baptism in Christ's blood.

The two latter versions represent, then, a combining in various ways of familiar elements. The chief point of this chapter has been our analysis of the relationship between the Seth and rood-tree legends when they made their first combined appearance in western Europe—presumably in the interpolated manuscripts of the *Vita*. The evidence points to the existence in Hebrew of a legend in which Seth brings a branch of the tree of life to Adam, of the translation of this story into Greek, of its being combined with *The Apocalypse of Moses*, of its Christianization by the inclusion first of material from *The Gospel of Nicodemus* and then the addition of rood-tree material, and finally its translation from Greek into Slavonic, Armenian, and Latin.

It would seem that there were in the West two forms of the rood-tree legend—one as in the Bodleian version and the other as in the Class III manuscripts of the *Vita*. The Slavonic legend of the three trees provides the closest extant analogue for both—the Bodleian version resembles the narrative of the second, or Eve's tree; the Class III manuscripts of the *Vita* resemble the accounts of both the third, or God's tree, and the first, or Adam's tree. Whether this Slavonic work was extant in Greek, it is impossible to say, and consequently whether the material came directly from the Greek or through a Slavonic intermediary is unknown.

This situation suggests the possibility that the rood-tree legend may have entered Western literature through at least two channels, that in the West there may have been at least two separate adaptations of the heretical material preserved in Slavonic—one form represented by the Bodleian version and the other by the interpolated *Vita*. Ultimately the two adaptations—plus a variety of other motifs —were to be recombined to form the fully developed Seth and rood-tree legend.

The Queen of Sheba prefers wading through the brook,
to walking over the holy wood

Chapter 6

THE GREEN TREE
AND
THE DRY

The Crucifixion

THE NUMBER of different ways in which the Seth and
rood-tree legends were joined indicates that the two
stories were believed to be essentially related: the Seth
legend expressed the yearning of man for a sign of his
redemption and the rood legend revealed the gradual fulfilment of this hope. Each combination was an experiment,
and none was completely effective. The successful fusion
of the two stories was achieved by an unknown Latin
writer, probably of the thirteenth century, whose version
Meyer referred to as the *Legende*.[1] How successful this
fusion was is attested by the considerable number of extant Latin manuscripts and the impressive number of

translations and adaptations of it in almost all the languages of Europe.[2]

The *Legende,* as a composite version, is made up mostly of elements which have appeared earlier. According to Meyer, it is based on the interpolated *Vita* and the versions of Geoffrey of Viterbo and of Jacobus de Voragine.[3] In the process of combining sources the author added as well as omitted material. The omissions tell us something of his structural and narrative skill, but his additions enable us to understand his theme better.

Meyer suggested that the author contrived certain elements, but it would be more accurate to say that he drew indirectly as well as directly on antecedent material, revealing his originality in the adaptation of traditional stories and motifs rather than in the contrivance of anything new. An analysis of the *Legende* should make this point clear.

Before summarizing this version, we should note that stylistically it differs from most of its predecessors. It has a more leisurely style than any other version except the *Vita* and the Bodleian. For instance, the characters are depicted more fully. The aged Adam (932 years old) is presented as tired of uprooting bramble bushes, weary of all the labors performed by the sweat of his body and mournful over the evils arising from his progeny. Contrasted to the old age of Adam is the youthfulness of Seth: his willingness to undertake the impossible journey, his gropings toward understanding the significance of what he sees, his sense of wonder as he beholds the vision of Paradise, the urgency with which he returns to his father. Moses is given some emotional expression: anger at the rebellion of the Chosen People, disappointment when God denies him entry into the promised land. David is permitted a fuller range of emotion: he sings and dances in jubilation as he finds the fragrant twigs; after his sin, he weeps and laments under the tree; he grieves at his failure to complete the Temple, and finally, he is resigned to the will of God.

The *Legende* is superior to other versions not only in characterization but in the ease with which the narrative moves through its long history. The material is always firmly in hand; everything is subservient to the theme; there is no storytelling for its own sake, none of the rambling structure found in so much of medieval narrative. Besides being richer in characterization and smoother in narrative than most earlier versions, the *Legende* also contains more vivid description, especially of the splendor of Paradise.

The author's use of symbols, whether conscious or unconscious, deserves analysis. Among the most important are the seared footprints, the withered tree, and the snake as symbols of sin and death; the baby in the tree and the seeds as symbols of rebirth. Of these we shall have more to say presently.

It is interesting to observe that the stylistic features which seem worthy of note appear mainly in the first part, in the Seth legend and in the beginning of the rood-tree section. It is in the Seth story that most of the significant changes and additions were made. As the story progressed, the author dealt less freely with his material; his task became not so much a matter of adapting and retelling as of combining divergent traditions. It seems to be this factor which accounts for the stylistic and structural superiority of the earlier sections. Unfortunately the full text of the *Legende* cannot be given here; the following summary must suffice.

After Adam had been expelled from Paradise, he implored God to be merciful and was promised that in the end of time he would be granted the oil of mercy. When he had reached the age of 932, weary of labor and sorrowful over the evils of his progeny, Adam bade Seth go to Paradise to get the promised oil. He directed Seth to go eastward to the head of the valley and follow a green path, marked by seared footsteps.

When Seth reached Paradise, he was astonished by its splendor. In answer to his request, the angel [cherubim] gave Seth three glimpses of Paradise. In his first vision he saw a beautiful garden, filled with shining fruit and flowers and singing birds. From a bright fountain in the middle of Paradise flowed four rivers: Physon, Gygon, Tygris, and Euphrates; above the fountain stood a tree, stripped of leaves and bark. In the second vision Seth saw a serpent entwined about the bare trunk. In his third vision he saw a tree elevated to Heaven, on the top of which was a newborn baby. The roots of the tree extended to Hell, where he recognized his brother Abel. Before Seth departed, the angel informed him that the baby was the Son of God, who would come in the fulness of time to efface the sin of the first parents, and that he would be the promised oil of mercy. The angel then gave Seth three seeds of the apple from which Adam had eaten and told the son to plant them under his father's tongue. The seeds would become three trees: a cedar, which by its height signified the Father; a cypress, which by its fragrance represented the sweetness of the Son; a pine, which with its many seeds signified the Holy Spirit. Seth returned and related to his father what had happened, whereupon Adam rejoiced. After his father's death, Seth placed the three seeds in Adam's mouth, and from the three seeds grew three twigs.

Moses, after leading his people across the Red Sea, discovered the twigs growing in the valley of Hebron. Proclaiming them to be a sign of the Trinity, he uprooted the twigs, carried them about the desert for forty years, and performed miracles with them. Before his death Moses buried the twigs at Mt. Thabor.

Later David was directed to this spot by the Holy Spirit and rejoiced to find the twigs. With them he cured many who were oppressed with disease. On returning to Jerusalem, David placed the twigs in a well, where overnight they took root and grew together into a single trunk. He built a wall around the tree and each year for thirty years placed a silver ring around its trunk. Under this tree David composed his penitential psalms. In further expiation for his sins he began building the Temple, but he was denied the joy of completing it, for, as God reminded him, he was a man of blood. After David's

The Quest of Seth

death, Solomon resumed the task of building the Temple. In the course of construction his builders attempted to use the tree, but however it was cut, it was always either too long or too short. Solomon then ordered that the wood be placed in the Temple.

There came one day a woman called Maximilla, who inadvertently sat on the wood. As her clothes burst into flames, she cried out to Jesus as Lord and God. She was stoned by the Jews for blasphemy and thus became the first martyr. The wood was then thrown into the *probatica piscina,* whereupon an angel stirred the water, and those who first bathed there were cured of their infirmities. When the Jews had seen the miracles, they dragged the beam from the pond and placed it over the flowing Siloe so that the treading of feet might stamp out its marvelous power. The beam lay as a bridge until Sibylla, Queen of the South, came to visit Solomon. Perceiving the holy quality of the wood, she crossed the torrent with bare feet and uttered a prophecy of Christ's coming. As the time of the Crucifixion approached, a third of the beam was cut to form the cross. On this wood Christ died for the salvation of man.[4]

Here then is the outline of the *Legende,* which formed the basis of so many later versions. Except for the first part, which has been largely reworked, there are no important new elements, only adaptations and combinations of earlier versions. We might explore first the changes which have been made in the Seth story beginning with what has been omitted from the account in the interpolated *Vita.*

1. Eve does not accompany Seth.
2. Seth does not meet the beast.
3. Seth is not given a twig. (There is, of course, no trace of the episode of Seth's dropping it in the Jordan.) Instead, he is given three seeds.

These omissions are not in themselves of much significance, but taken together they indicate the selective method of the author; he eliminated details which were not relevant to his purpose. More important are the motifs which he added; these correspond to the points he wished to stress:

1. The withered footprints.
2. The three glimpses of Paradise.
   a) The dry tree.
   b) The snake in the dry tree.
   c) The baby in the great tree.

The withered footprints are the most important feature of the journey: other details have been added which are a commonplace in twelfth- and thirteenth-century accounts of journeys to the Earthly Paradise. As Howard Rollin Patch remarks, "By the twelfth century, the idea of the Earthly Paradise was fairly well established in many respects."[5] First, as to its location, it is in the East,[6] and it is cut off from the rest of the world by its high altitude. Although usually on a high mountain, in the *Legende* it is at the head of a valley: the notion of the mountain as a barrier is not present in the *Legende:* the head of the valley suggests only a distant and lofty place.[7]

The withered footsteps, however, are not a stock motif. According to the *Legende,* when Adam and Eve were driven from Paradise, their footprints scorched a path in the earth and, where they walked, no grass ever grew. Although this element does not appear in precisely this form in any earlier work known to me, it bears a close resemblance to two widely spread folklore motifs: (1) that wrongdoing, usually murder, has a blighting effect on vegetation and (2) that footprints have magical significance. The belief in the withering effect of sin on vegetation was probably first related to the magical power attributed to blood. In one of the most common forms of the motif, grass will not grow where a man has been murdered.[8] Also widespread in folklore is the belief that no grass grows on the grave of a murderer.[9] This motif of the blighting effect of wrongdoing on vegetation is sometimes combined with the belief that footsteps have magical

The Quest of Seth

significance.[10] These two notions appear together in the Welsh Triads: where Llew Llaw Gyffes, one of the three crimson-stained ones, trod, neither herb nor grass sprang up for a year.[11] There is probably no knowing for certain the source of this motif of the withered footsteps, but it evidently impressed not only our author (it is repeated in a variant form as the dry tree) but almost all succeeding compilers of the legend. The likelihood is that he adapted a folklore motif to suit his purpose, which here seems to have been to portray vividly and dramatically the permanent consequences of the sin of Adam and Eve. The withered footsteps serve both to lead Seth to Paradise and to emphasize the blighting effect of original sin.

The journey of Seth in the *Legende,* unlike the journey of the typical hero, is not fraught with danger. Unlike Gilgamesh, who faces towering mountains, Seth has only to ascend to the head of a valley; there are no scorpion-people like those whom Gilgamesh encountered, and the beast whom Eve and Seth met in *The Apocalypse of Moses* has disappeared. For Seth there is no tunnel of darkness, no water of death.[12] Even the Jordan into which the Seth of the interpolated *Vita* dropped his twig on his return journey has been omitted. For Seth there are only the scorched footprints to remind him of the permanent blight caused by the sin of his parents. The fiery wall which surrounds Paradise appears to most heroes as a dangerous barrier, but to Seth it is a splendid sight.[13] The cherubim with flaming swords[14] have become a helpful angel who gives him three glimpses into Paradise and then three seeds.

We might observe that up to this point Seth's journey has been a real though not a dangerous journey; it has not been a part of a vision; on the contrary, the vision which he sees is a part of his journey. F. C. Burkitt notes that there are essentially two kinds of visions, the "real visions, i.e., pictures seen by the writer in dream or ecstasy" and the "so-called visions" which "read like conscious inventions; every detail in them is completely and satisfactorily explained."[15] The vision of Seth is more nearly of the latter sort. The images which Seth sees have been deliberately chosen by the author, and their significance is clearly pointed out.

Seth's vision consists of three parts: the three glimpses which he is given of Paradise. His first glance is rather comprehensive; it takes in the whole span of Paradise and then focuses on the dry tree. Before examining the nature of this tree, we should consider its setting. The hero's vision of Paradise is, of course, a standard motif in myths and legends, and the objects which Seth sees correspond closely to those seen by the traditional hero: fruit, flowers, singing birds, radiance, a fountain from which flow four great streams of water and above it a marvelous tree.[16] It is the tree which compels Seth's attention in this and in his subsequent glimpses of Paradise. It is in the author's handling of the marvelous tree (traditionally the tree of knowledge or life) that he has worked most freely and creatively.

The first vision, in which Seth beholds the dry tree, we mentioned earlier in connection with the withered footsteps. Here it is the tree, rather than the grass, which suffers the blighting effect of wrongdoing. Both motifs may have the same ultimate origin in man's realization of the blighting consequences of sin, but, whereas the dry footsteps appear chiefly in folklore, the dry tree appeared in early literary traditions and continued to reappear widely, both before and after the *Legende* was written.[17]

The motif of the dry tree is widespread, but it will be considered here only in terms of its origin and its appearance in those works which, even if not sources, represent the same line of tradition which we find in the *Legende*. In what seems to be its earliest literary appearance the dry tree is placed, as it frequently is in later literature, in relation to the green tree: in Ezechiel 17:24, "all the trees of the country shall know that I the Lord have . . . dried

The Quest of Seth

up the green tree, and have caused the dry tree to flour-ish."[18] The dry tree and the green tree here symbolize the power of God to reverse the forces of nature, to destroy the flourishing and to resurrect the dead. The idea that vegetation withers because of sin is present here, as well as in the motif of the dry footsteps, but the emphasis is different: the withering of the green tree is not so much a direct consequence of sin as a sign to man of God's power and wrath. M. R. Bennett believes it is possible that there was an allegory of the green tree and the dry, in part of Jewish origin, which was in some form well known at the time of Christ.[19] She mentions the passage in Luke 23:31 in which Jesus, during the procession to Calvary, referred to the green tree and the dry.[20]

The belief that blight is the consequence of sin appears also in *The Apocalypse of Moses:* after the disobedience of Adam and Eve, all the trees except the tree of knowledge (a fig tree) shed their leaves.[21] Reminiscent both of Ezechiel's prophecy and the passage in *The Apocalypse of Moses* are the words which Jesus addressed to a fig tree in Matthew 21:18: "Let no fruit ever grow on thee here-after; whereupon the fig tree withered away."[22]

In the Ethiopian *Book of Adam and Eve* (fifth to sixth century) it is the tree of knowledge that withers at the Fall. Adam was shown the tree before leaving the garden, and it had become dry.[23]

In an Egyptian work, entitled "The Mysteries of St. John the Apostle" (the MS is dated 1006), the tree of knowledge is also represented as bare because of the sin of Adam.[24] Here the tree appears in the seventh heaven and is shown to John by the cherubim who has taken him there. His translation reminds one of Enoch's, of Jonitus' in Geoffrey of Viterbo's version (note the similarity in names, John and Jonitus), and Seth's in the interpolated *Liber Floridus.*[25] It is impossible to explore the matter fully here, but one cannot but be struck by the possible significance of these parallels. Here is the earliest, indeed, as far as I know, the only other work in which a figure with the cherubim for a guide, sees in a vision of Paradise the dry tree, which is identified as the tree of knowledge.

The dry tree is also found very early in the development of the Alexander romances. One of the most elaborate accounts appears in the Syriac version of the Pseudo-Callisthenes (fifth–tenth centuries).[26] Here the dry tree stands, not in the luxuriant growth of Paradise, as in the Ethiopian *Book of Adam and Eve* and the *Legende*, but in a wasteland. The tree is intended to reveal, as Rose Jeffries Peebles observes, death to the hero. There is, moreover, a phoenix on the top of the dry tree. We shall refer again to the phoenix in the tree since he corresponds to the baby in the tree, which Seth sees in his third vision; both probably symbolize resurrection.[27] The dry tree with the phoenix in its branches appears also in the Latin version of the Alexander romance which was widely known throughout Europe in the Middle Ages, the *Historia de Preliis*, translated by the Archpriest Leo in the tenth century.[28]

Although the exact source from which the author of the *Legende* drew the motif of the dry tree cannot at this time be determined, the most significant analogues seem to be the Egyptian "Mysteries of St. John the Apostle" and the tenth-century Latin translation of the Alexander romance. The former represents the closer parallel, but no case for borrowing can be established until lines of transmission are laid down. The latter, although more accessible to our author, is a less exact parallel. In both works the dry tree is seen in a vision and has symbolic significance: in the Alexander romance it symbolizes death; in the Egyptian work it symbolizes sin and death.

As Miss Peebles observes, "In the thirteenth century the legend of the Dry Tree was extraordinarily popular."[29] But its many appearances in the travel romances of the time represent a different tradition, or perhaps, as Miss Peebles indicates, a literal interpretation of the symbolical tradition. The symbol was taken to be a concrete fact, an ac-

112

tual tree to be visited by voyagers.[30] The dry tree in the travel literature was no longer a symbol, an object seen in a vision of Paradise, but a geographical entity to be found on a map and visited. For instance, according to Marco Polo (*ca.* 1254–1324), the dry tree was located in a province called Tonocain, at the extemity of Persia toward the North.[31] A somewhat different tradition appears in Odoric de Pordenone (1286–1331), where the dry tree is located on the mount of Mamre. Unlike the tree in the *Legende,* which died at the sin of Adam, it died when Christ was crucified.[32] A similar account appears in Mandeville, who probably took it from Odoric.[33] On the thirteenth-century Hereford map the location of the dry tree in the Terrestrial Paradise reflects the two current attitudes toward it: the belief in its geographical existence and a lingering interest in its symbolical significance.

An important link between the dry tree of travel literature and the dry tree of the Seth legend is noted by Friedrich Zarncke in his study of Prester John. He quotes from a Cambridge manuscript of the *Epistola Presbyteri Johannis* (*ca.* 1300) a passage in which the Christians ask Prester John about the *arbor sicca* and are told that it is the *arbor Seth.*[34] We probably have here the influence of the Seth legend upon the tradition of the dry tree. One wonders if the reverse might not also be true, that the dry-tree legend influenced the Seth legend. The similarity in the names, especially in French, *arbre sec* and *arbre Seth,* suggests the possibility that pre-existent traditions of *arbre sec* might have suggested the connection with the Seth legend. Eleanor Simmons Greenhill, referring to Adolf Jacoby as her source, mentions that the dry tree had been identified with the cross since the time of Godfrey (Geoffrey) of Viterbo (d. 1196).[35] In Godfrey, the tree of which the cross was made is referred to as *arbor sicca,* but it is clear that the tree was called dry because the pond in which it had been lying had dried up.[36] It seems doubtful that this tree, dry because it was no longer wet, is to be identified with the withered tree of Seth's vision. Reference to the tree as *arbor sicca* may, however, have suggested to a later compiler the connection with the traditional *arbre sec*.

The whole point—the relationship between the Seth legend and the tradition of the dry tree—needs more exploration than is possible here. But it seems reasonably clear that from the powerful imagery of Ezechiel several traditions emerged. It was the symbolical tradition which the author of the *Legende* drew upon, the tradition in which the dry tree was the symbol of death, and more specifically of the death brought into the world by the Fall of Man. Although the image of the dry tree is an exceedingly old one, the significance attached to it in its earliest appearance in Ezechiel is not essentially different from its meaning in the *Legende.* The use of the dry tree by the author made it henceforth an integral part of the Seth and rood-tree legend. The dry tree also continued to be incorporated into different types of later medieval literature from travel romances to religious allegories.[37]

It was inevitable that the dry tree, a real object in the visible world, devoid of leaves and bark, bleached white, dead, yet standing, an arresting image, should have been used as a symbol for those elusive mysteries, sin and death. It is not surprising that the dry tree should appear so often, over long periods of time, in many languages, and in different types of literature. In its mingled familiarity and strangeness it elicits a universal response as a figure of death.

As for its use in the *Legende,* we might conclude by saying that the dry tree symbolizes the blight caused by the sin of Adam and Eve. Like the dry footsteps, it is a sign to Seth (and to all men) of the change which took place in nature with the Fall of Man.

Seth's next glimpse of Paradise reveals essentially the same point: the serpent entwined about the dry tree also represents the sin and consequent death of man. The serpent is among the most ancient and widespread symbols, but it differs from the dry tree in having numerous meanings attached to it. It has symbolized life, healing, wisdom, immortality, and it has symbolized evil and death. These various manifestations represent the beneficent and malevolent aspects of the serpent and can be related to two basic attitudes, each of which has been viewed in two distinct ways: the serpent as an embodiment of the life force, especially the male principle, has been an object of worship; in the same capacity it has been made to represent matter and has been placed in unfavorable contrast to the bird, representing spirit. The belief of primitive man that serpents cast their skins and so live forever has similarly resulted in two quite different attitudes: a veneration of the serpent as immortal and a hostility toward him as the usurper of a right intended for man.[38] This latter belief is reflected in the basic Judeo-Christian use of the symbol as found in Genesis—the serpent as the cause of man's alienation from God. This is the primary interpretation to be placed on the serpent which Seth sees.[39]

The serpent in the *Legende* is, as in Genesis, closely related to the tree of knowledge. This relationship between serpent and tree is a commonplace in mythology with analogues present in most cultures.[40] Although found almost universally, the motif, like that of the serpent itself, has had many different meanings attached to it. For instance, among primitive peoples the serpent coiled about the tree symbolized fertility. In Greek myth the serpent entwined about the sacred tree was the guardian, usually of the golden apples of Hera in the garden of the Hesperides. In Nordic mythology the serpent at the roots of the tree, Yggdrasil, symbolized the evil forces which would destroy the tree. In the story which Frazer relates of how the serpent deprived mankind of the gift of immortality, the tree also occupied a central place. The serpent deceived man by recommending that he eat of the tree of life (actually the tree of death), and thus man became subject to death, but the serpent, who ate of the tree of life, became immortal.[41] In the Genesis account, the serpent is the tempter; he tempts man to disobey his creator by eating of the tree of "knowledge." It is clearly the biblical meaning which the author of the *Legende* intended in Seth's vision of the serpent entwined about the tree: the serpent signifies the Temptation and Fall of Man and the entrance of Death into the world.

The motif of the serpent coiled about the tree trunk is not only the product of a literary tradition; it also figures conspicuously in art. It appears on Phoenician coins,[42] on Greek vases,[43] on bowls of the Sassanian period (seventh century, Persian).[44] The precise meaning of the motif of the serpent encircling the tree on ancient artifacts is not beyond dispute; the serpent may be a fertilizing agent, a guardian of the tree, or a tempter. The form of the motif, however, remained strikingly the same, not only in ancient but in Christian times. The motif of the serpent entwined about the tree is a commonplace in Christian art, making its earliest appearance in the catacombs and reaching its fullest representation in the twelfth and thirteenth centuries.[45] Among the countless examples of the motif are those on sarcophagi at Rome, dated fourth or fifth century, and on a Sicilian bas-relief of the Cathedral at Monreale.[46] The representation on Christian monuments of the serpent coiled about the tree clearly illustrates the theme of the Temptation. And so with the serpent encircling the tree in the *Legende*. Although the form of the motif had been established centuries earlier, its meaning was provided by the Judeo-Christian tradition; it illustrated the great theme of medieval Christendom, the Temptation and Fall of Man.[47] We have then the same image used to represent widely dissimilar ideas; a symbol of naturalistic origin, used in a later period to embody a metaphysical concept. The form remained unchanged, but the ideas which animated the form changed in accordance with the beliefs of the time.

In none of these representations—artistic or literary—is the serpent coiled about a dry tree. This combination of the two images of death—the dry tree and the serpent— seems to be the contribution of the *Legende*. Surely the use of the two symbols, one encircling the other, strengthens the effect; the total impression is of the serpent exultant in the midst of the death to which he has brought man.

In his third glimpse of Paradise, Seth sees a tree whose branches reach Heaven and whose roots extend into Hell. On the top of the tree is a newborn baby, wrapped in swaddling clothes. We have here actually two elements: the tree itself and the child at its summit. We shall consider first the child in the tree, a motif which also appears in several of the grail romances. In Wauchier's continuation of Chrétien's *Perceval* (1190–1200), the hero sees a great tree; sitting in the branches is a beautiful child, around five years of age, handsomely dressed, holding an apple. After a brief exchange with Perceval the child climbs the tree and disappears.[48] In the *Didot Perceval* (early thirteenth century) the hero sees in the tree two children, naked, about seven years old.[49] In *Durmart le Gallois* (first quarter of the thirteenth century) the hero sees a tree with one child, who later appears wounded in five places.[50]

The appearance of the child in the tree in Arthurian romance has resulted in a number of investigations of this motif. The first of these, by Jessie L. Weston, attempts to relate the episodes to a mystery play based on pre-Christian apple-tree rituals.[51] Miss Weston's article has not been favorably received and is generally less pertinent to the Seth legend than to the grail legends.[52] Two years later an article by Miss Peebles appeared in which she suggested that the child in Wauchier be compared "with the child Jesus in the tree in the thirteenth-century vision of Seth."[53] Miss Peebles, however, was more interested in the two children in the *Didot Perceval* version and found the most significant parallels, if not actual sources, in the sun and moon trees of the Alexander romance.[54] More relevant to Seth's vision was Brugger's study. Brugger, impressed by the similarity between Seth's vision and Perceval's adventure (in Wauchier), assumed that the former had influenced the latter.[55] He was also aware of the marked differences, and these he attributed to pagan influence in the form of the dwarf-king, Alberich-Auberon.[56] Mrs. Greenhill has twice written on the motif of the child in the tree. In her thesis on the episode in Wauchier she states, following Brugger's lead: "It will be the business of this essay to account for the presence of pagan material in this episode as well as to establish the presence of influence from the Seth legend."[57] Mrs. Greenhill's chief efforts are devoted to pointing out Celtic parallels. She may be right in her conclusion that the origin of the child in the tree episode in the Arthurian romances (especially in Wauchier) is in pagan Celtic traditions of the other world,[58] but one problem remains: the dwarfs whom she mentions as resembling the child are always under the tree, never in it. She is forced to conclude that "who first placed the child in the tree is of course a mystery."[59] She refers to Professor Loomis' suggestion that there was a possibility of manuscript corruption, a confusion between *soz* ("beneath") and *sor* ("above"). Scribal error is, of course, a possible explanation; the likelihood of "error" is increased, however, when there is a pre-existent tradition which renders the change meaningful.[60]

It is conceivable that a manuscript change, whether accidental or intentional, might account for Wauchier's child in the tree, but it is exceedingly unlikely that it could account for the baby in the tree in Seth's vision. The chief qualities which relate the dwarfs to Wauchier's child—rich dress, beauty, refusal to speak freely to Perceval, giving directions to Perceval—are lacking in the baby whom Seth saw in the tree. Indeed, Mrs. Greenhill herself implies an independent origin of the Seth episode when she concludes, as Brugger does, that Seth's vision was assimilated with that of Perceval.[61]

Evidently, however, Mrs. Greenhill was not totally convinced of the conclusions she had reached in her thesis. In 1954, in her article, "The Child in the Tree," she first points out Brugger's mistake in assuming that the child in the tree episodes in Arthurian romance were influenced by Seth's vision.[62] The *Legende*, as Meyer indicates, was composed in the last quarter of the thirteenth century, some seventy-five years later than Wauchier's continuation.[63] In this paper Mrs. Greenhill attempts "to show that Wauchier had ample . . . precedent in Christian tradition on which to base the child-in-the-tree episode."[64] She cites a formidable array of Christian works which she believes represent the tradition from which Wauchier's child in the tree came. She places the emphasis almost entirely on the tree as a cosmological tree, especially in its role as a ladder. Mrs. Greenhill performed a service in pointing out the error of Brugger's theory and in bringing together a great deal of material on the appearance of the cosmological tree in Christian sources. Finally, however, whether the child in Wauchier was, as Mrs. Greenhill earlier thought, derived from Celtic dwarfs or, as she later believed, from representations of the soul ascending the ladder of virtue, is not for us to decide here. But one feels, after reading these studies, that the essential mystery of the child in the tree—whether in Wauchier, *Didot-Perceval, Durmart,* or in the Seth legend—remains unsolved. As Mrs. Greenhill admitted, "these episodes have little in common and show a knowledge of traditions which we have not been able to treat in this paper."[65] Whatever Mrs. Greenhill may have had in mind, I think she is right in suggesting that other traditions may supply the answer to the mystery of the child in the tree.

Although there may well be a relationship between Seth's vision and the visions of the grail heroes, the differences are marked, especially in the case of Perceval in

Wauchier and in the *Didot-Perceval*. More closely resembling the baby whom Seth sees is the child of Durmart's vision. As the *Legende*, according to the present state of evidence, is considerably later than *Durmart*,[66] and as it is inherently improbable that the *Legende* could have been influenced by *Durmart*, the only reasonable conclusion at this time is that each drew independently on preexisting traditions.

However interesting the general motif of the child in the tree and its appearance in the grail romances, our chief purpose is to account for the baby of Seth's vision. Although the explanation which follows may also be relevant to the grail episodes, a separate study would be required to trace the relationships fully.

One of the most obvious differences between the *Legende* and Wauchier accounts is that Perceval sees a child: whether its prototype was a dwarf or a soul, it remains a mysterious child. Seth sees a baby wrapped in swaddling clothes who, whatever its prototype, is the infant Jesus. Further, the small baby on the top of the great tree is a symbol, whereas the child in the branches is a character who speaks and moves. Seth's vision is not like that of Perceval, an episode; it is an image, something seen. This exclusively visual nature of Seth's experience suggests the possibility of iconographical influence. One wonders, for instance, whether the widely represented tree of Jesse could have influenced the form of Seth's vision. Certain parallels at once suggest themselves: the tree with Christ at the top and a figure beneath (Jesse might be comparable to Abel whom Seth saw at the roots of the tree). Certain differences also suggest themselves: the tree of Jesse is usually highly formalized, complex, and overlaid, whereas the tree of Seth's vision is simple. Arthur Watson, however, points out that the earliest forms of the tree of Jesse are simple, that a typical early form (eleventh and early twelfth century) would consist of Jesse, the rod represented by Mary, with Christ at the top.[67] Another

The Quest of Seth

difference between the tree of Jesse and the tree of Seth's vision is less readily dismissed: the former is a genealogical tree; the latter, it is generally agreed, is cosmological.[68]

The cosmological tree, like the tree of Jesse, also appears in the Old Testament in passages which were interpreted as Messianic prophecies.[69] In Ezechiel 17:22–24 there is a great cedar from whose top branches the Lord says he will crop off a tender twig and plant it on a high mountain, and in Daniel 4:7–14 Nebuchadnezzar beheld in his dream "a tree in the midst of the earth" "and the height thereof reached unto heaven." But there is no baby in the top of these trees. Nor in any case known to me is the Christ portrayed at the top of the tree of Jesse, a baby, unless he is with his mother;[70] otherwise he is represented as fully grown.[71] Although I would not entirely abandon this possibility, we must conclude reluctantly that the source of the child in the tree motif is to be sought in other traditions, probably more ancient.

There are essentially two motifs in Seth's vision: the child in the tree and the great tree extending its branches into heaven and stretching its roots into the underworld. Although the two are essentially separate, one can find traces of their being joined in the earliest traditions—both literary and pictorial—of Egypt and Babylonia. For instance, in Egypt the cosmic tree was originally conceived as a celestial tree from whose summit the sun god rose each morning.[72] As the mistress of heaven, Hat-hôr was believed to have been identical to the celestial tree;[73] she was called "the Lady of the Sycamore" and it was she who daily gave birth to the young sun god.[74] An illustration provided by W. Max Müller shows Osiris, as "the lord of resurrection and of new and eternal life," in the midst of the celestial tree.[75]Sometimes it is the soul of Osiris, represented as a phoenix, which rests on the sacred tree.[76] The Egyptian sun god, Ra, was also depicted emerging from a tree, the sycamore, representing the mother-goddess.[77]

The Green Tree and the Dry

Paralleling the Egyptian forms of the motif are the Babylonian. On cylinder seals of the second millennium appears a conventionalized representation: a winged disc hovering over the sacred tree.[78] More explicit is the treatment of the theme in the fragment of an old bilingual hymn: in Eridu (Babylonian tradition placed the garden of Eden in the immediate vicinity of Eridu) a stalk grew; its root stretched toward the deep; its foliage was the couch of the primeval mother; in the midst of it was Tammuz, the sun, her child.[79] Here the cosmological nature of the tree is unmistakable as well as the identification of the tree with the mother-goddess and her child, the sun god.

A striking form of this motif is depicted on a marble altar from Palmyra (Syria). On the back of the altar the sun god, Malak-Bêl, portrayed as a naked boy, issues from the top of a cypress tree, bearing on his shoulders a ram (also a sun symbol).[80] According to René Dussaud, the scene represents the birth of the young god, Malak-Bêl, from the tree. Dussaud relates the figure of Malak-Bêl with that of Hermes Criophore,[81] which in turn provided the model for early representations of the Good Shepherd.[82] Dussaud also points out, as a parallel to Malak-Bêl's birth from the cypress, the myth of Adonis, who was born after his mother, Myrrha or Smyrna, had been transformed into a tree.[83] In Lebanon, Venus bore the local name of the cypress, and the story is told that Apuleius, wishing to paint the son of Venus in his mother's lap, represented him in the foliage of the cypress.[84]

As we have seen then, the cosmological tree appears in the art and literature of ancient Egypt and Babylonia; in both traditions the tree is identified with the sky goddess (later the earth goddess), and in both the sun god is represented emerging from the top. The sun god may be depicted as a radiating disc, as a youth, or as a phoenix. We have also observed a Syrian representation of the sun god, with a ram on his shoulders, rising from a cypress tree. This figure bearing the ram appeared frequently in Greek art and served as a model for Christian representations of the Good Shepherd.

The motif of the god in the tree appeared in Christian art in varying forms: at least once as a ram at the top of the tree of life,[85] more often as a phoenix on the top of a tree, usually a palm.[86] In one case known to me, a head (believed to be Christ's) appears at the apex of the tree of life.[87] On the Countess of Joigny's tomb there is a very fine piece of sculpture, dated early thirteenth century, which depicts a youth standing amid the branches of a tree, generally identified as the tree of life. Although it has been suggested that the sculpture illustrates a story in *Barlaam and Josaphat,* it very much resembles the representation of Osiris in the tree. Moreover, the figure itself resembles not a hunter (as in the story in *Barlaam and Josaphat*) but the youthful Christ. Although the identification of the figure is uncertain, the representation on a tomb of a young boy in the midst of the tree of life suggests that it was intended as a symbol of rebirth.[88]

An extremely interesting survival of this motif of the young god (sun god, Christ) in the tree has been reproduced by Louisa Twining from a book of illuminations in the British Museum, dated about 1400.[89] Here a serpent is entwined about the trunk of a tree and in the top Christ appears as a young man with a nimbus. The illustration combines quite closely the second and third of Seth's visions.

Thus far we have been considering the motif of the sun god in the tree, though it must be admitted that we have encountered no instance of a baby at the summit. We shall return to this point, but meanwhile should consider more closely the cosmological tree. As we have seen, the young sun god traditionally emerged from the cosmological tree, though in some instances, especially in connection with the mother-goddess, the tree lacks clear signs of being cosmological and suggests rather the tree of life. As Widengren observes, the tree of life and the cosmic tree "may from time to time be identified but may also be kept apart."[90]

We have noted the great antiquity of the concept of the cosmic tree and its appearance in the Old Testament.[91] As Mrs. Greenhill shows, it continued to be represented in Christian art and literature where it was often brought into relationship with the cross.[92] Mrs. Greenhill assumes that the cosmological tree which Seth saw was the cross and that the baby represented the crucified Christ.[93] Although it is perfectly clear that the baby is Christ, it is less clear that he represents Christ crucified or that the tree represents solely, or even primarily, the cross. The imagery of Seth's vision does not suggest the Crucifixion. The great tree is a world tree and a tree of life. Admittedly the tree of life was often associated with the cross,[94] but the figure on the tree of the cross is the dying God, not a newborn infant.

I should like, therefore, to suggest another possible interpretation of the baby in the tree, the subject of Seth's third vision. The tree of life was interpreted in Christian thought not only as the cross but as Christ himself and, more important for us, as the Virgin Mother.[95] By the twelfth century the cult of the Virgin had assumed vast proportions and evoked intense fervor.[96] The hymn-writers, in their efforts to praise the Mother of God, drew upon the rich imagery of the Old Testament. "To her were applied the verses of Ecclesiasticus 24:17: 'I was exalted like a cedar in Libanus, as a cypress on Mount Sion: I was exalted like a palm tree in Cades . . . as a fair olive tree in the plains.' "[97] The *Psalterium beatae Mariae V* of Edmund of Canterbury (*ca.* 1170–1240) opens with these lines:

> Ave, virgo, lignum mite,
> Quae dedisti fructum vitae
> Saluti fidelium.[98]

Bonaventura (1221–74) saluted the mother of Jesus thus:

> Ave, Virgo, vitae lignum
> Quae perenni laude dignum,
> Salvo voto, quod vovisti,
> Mundo fructum attulisti.[99]

Although one may grant the metaphorical identity of the tree of life to her who bore "the light of the world," we must return to the point that in no earlier sources—literary or pictorial—have we found the motif of the newborn baby at the top of a tree.

In the absence of any prior appearance we might assume that the author of the *Legende* did something remarkable for the Middle Ages; he created something new. In the process he drew upon tradition—the tradition of a deity in the tree, represented as a child or a phoenix, and he transformed the figure into the infant Jesus. Symbolically speaking, what was more natural, if the tree of life represented the Virgin Mother, than to place the infant Jesus in the foliage? But this was a startling and daring innovation, to take the baby in swaddling clothes, usually depicted only in nativity scenes, sheltered and surrounded by adoring figures, and place him alone on the top of the cosmic tree. The innovation is surprising but right. For this is not the Nativity, but a prefiguration of the Nativity, revealed to Seth's wondering gaze in brilliant symbolism. How fitting a symbol of rebirth! How right that the prefiguration should appear in the ancient and universal form of the Virgin Mother, represented as a tree of life, bearing her divine son. The idea grows on one that the primary meaning of the great tree of Seth's vision is the great mother, bearing the baby who is to be the savior of the world. The symbol combines the tree of life, with the infant redeemer, and the cosmic tree, which relates Heaven, Earth, and Hell, and provides a means of ascent for the soul of the just Abel. Perhaps obscurely, the cross bearing the divine savior may be prefigured, for finally redemption was achieved not by his birth but by his death. But the glowing imagery of Seth's vision brings the joyful promise of the Messiah; there is no sign of the stark reality of the Crucifixion.

We have observed the similarity not only in imagery but in significance between the ancient representations of the young sun god emerging from the cosmic tree and the infant Jesus at the top of the world tree.[100] We have finally to establish the relationship, if any, between them.

Goblet d'Alviella describes "a symbolism so natural that . . . it does not belong to any definite region or race, but constitutes a characteristic feature of humanity." He cites, as examples, the representation of the sun by a disc, of the moon by a crescent, of water by fishes or by a wavy line. He adds that there are "certain more complicated analogies": the tree of life, the divine triad, and the four directions of space or the cross.[101] Goblet d'Alviella does not mention the motif of the baby in the tree. Whether or not he would assign this motif to his category of "more complicated analogies" is a matter of conjecture. His general conclusion is "that the religious symbols common to the different . . . races of mankind have not originated independently among them, but have, for the most part, been carried from one to the other, in the course of their migrations, conquests, and commerce."[102]

On the other hand, Jung refers to "the host of images, which are to be found in the mythologies of all ages and all peoples. The sum of these images constitutes the collective unconscious, a heritage which is potentially present in every individual."[103] Jung believes that the concept of birth from trees is one of the "archetypes of the collective unconscious."[104]

Unlike the image of the serpent entwined in the tree, which appeared frequently in pagan and Christian culture, the baby in the tree appears in the form in which Seth saw it in no other source known to me. The symbol which Seth saw was not a conventional one, though it was a variation on an ancient motif. Whether it was a survival of a primitive symbol, taken from an unknown source, or remodeled from a more conventional image, or a brilliant creation of the author, an image tossed up from the "collective unconscious," cannot finally be known. In any case, the motif reveals a sure instinct for the right symbol; it is a striking image which combines the familiar and the strange in such a way as to suggest an authentic vision.

In conclusion, one might say that the framework of Seth's visions was contrived to fit the theological conceptions of the time—the representation of the past transgression and of the future redemption—but the forms of the visions were ancient, pre-Christian. The first two visions which Seth sees are conventional symbols of sin and death —the dry tree and the serpent entwined about the tree— but the third glimpse of Paradise, which symbolizes rebirth, may belong to the realm of authentic vision in which diverse elements are brought together to form a new pattern. Seth's last glimpse is a visual representation of the verbal prophecy which first appeared in *The Gospel of Nicodemus*. It represents the fully developed as well as the Christianized form of Seth's quest for the oil of mercy. For Seth the fulfilment of the quest is the promise, revealed in ancient and splendid imagery, of the Christ, the oil of mercy, who will come from the Virgin Mother, the tree of life.

As Seth leaves Paradise, the angel gives him three seeds of the fruit from which Adam had eaten. At this point the legend of the rood-tree begins. In the three seeds which the angel gives Seth and instructs him to plant in Adam's mouth, we recognize an adaptation of the one seed which the angel planted in the mouth of Adam in the interpolated *De imagine mundi* and the three twigs of the Bodleian and other versions.[105]

In both the *De imagine mundi* version and the *Legende* the seed or seeds come from the tree of knowledge, though in the latter the tree is further identified as the apple. The widespread supposition that the forbidden fruit was an apple has been traced by Kaufman Kohler to the Targum translation of "tappuah" in Canticles 2:3 and 7:9 as "tappuah di gintha di Eden" ("paradise-apple").[106] Aquila and later Jerome interpreted the apple tree of Canticle 8:5 as the tree of knowledge.[107] The frequent use of the apple in Christian symbolism to represent the fall was probably reinforced by representations of Hercules with the apples of the Hesperides and the serpent wound around the tree.[108] The mention of the apple in the *Legende* is extraneous,[109] even awkward, however, since it is related that from the seeds come cedar, cypress, and pine sprouts! At this point too many traditions have been unskilfully combined.

In the suceeding sections the author has drawn upon material which we have already considered: Moses saw the twigs as a sign of the Trinity, performed miracles with them, and finally planted them. These episodes are closely paralleled in the Bodleian account. Meyer, being unacquainted with this early English version, supposes them to have been contrived, or taken from an unknown source.[110]

The next section relates David's finding the twigs, his performing cures, his planting the twigs in Jerusalem where they became one tree, and his placing a silver ring about the tree each year for thirty years. Meyer believes that for this account of David and the tree the author was dependent on Geoffrey.[111] But all these incidents are more closely paralleled in the Bodleian version than in Geoffrey.

The following sections relate the history of the wood under Solomon. For this history there were contradictory narratives.[112] What the author of the *Legende* did was to combine them. As Meyer points out, the author probably used the interpolated *Vita* and Geoffrey for his account of Solomon's attempt to use the wood in building the Temple and its being placed in the completed edifice. The Bodleian version contains a similar account.

The next episode tells of Maximilla. When she sat on

128   *The Quest of Seth*

the wood, her clothes burst into flame, and she called to Jesus with a prophetic voice. She was stoned and became the first martyr. Meyer once again attributes to Geoffrey an episode which bears a much closer resemblance to one in the Bodleian version. The name Maximilla is new, however, occurring in no earlier version known to me. It is an uncommon name; as far as I have been able to discover, there has been only one saint called Maximilla. She was one of twelve martyrs in Africa of whom very little is known.[113] In the apocryphal *Acts of Andrew* there appears a lady called Maximilla, who is converted by Andrew, but no indication is given either of prophecy or martyrdom.[114] Of more relevance is a Montanist prophetess of this name, described by Hippolytus, Tertullian, and Eusebius.[115] She was accused of prophesying in a state of ecstatic frenzy and of extending the heresy of Montanus among the Phrygians. She was believed to have been martyred around 179. It was probably this Maximilla whose name was given to the prophesying martyr of the *Legende*. We have then an episode closely resembling one which we met in the Bodleian version, though the fact that the woman is called Maximilla from the start rather than Susanna after her conversion, suggests that the *Legende* author was drawing on an earlier form of the Bodleian version.[116]

The next element, that the tree was thrown into the *probatica piscina* where it effected cures, has been too recurrent a motif to need further comment.

The following section relates that the Jews, angered by the miracles which occurred in the *probatica piscina*, dragged the wood from the pond and made of it a bridge across the flowing Siloe.[117] Meyer ascribes this episode to Jacobus de Voragine's *Legenda Aurea*, but the account in Johannes Beleth's *Rationale divinorum officiorum* (*ca.* 1170) is essentially the same and considerably earlier. Meyer gives no evidence that the *Legende* author used Jacobus rather than Beleth;[118] indeed, as Meyer himself indicates, Jacobus was using Beleth's version. In both it is related that Solomon, angered by his failure to use the wood in the construction of the Temple, had it used as a bridge. The account in Beleth and Jacobus resembles the one in the *Legende* in that the wood is used as a bridge, but whereas in Beleth-Jacobus the wood is taken from the Temple, in the *Legende* it is taken from the *probatica piscina*. Which source the author of the *Legende* used is of less relevance than the fact that he adapted antecedent material to suit his purpose, which was to combine the two different traditions of the prophesying sibyl. The sibyl who found the wood in the Temple became Maximilla; the sibyl who found the wood as a bridge became the Queen of Sheba. In the *Legende,* as in Beleth, the queen came to Jerusalem and, finding the wood used as a bridge, adored it and crossed the torrent with bare feet. The prophecy which she uttered, however, is from the Eighth Book of the *Sibylline Oracles,* as in the interpolated *De imagine mundi.*[119]

Finally, in the *Legende,* as in the Bodleian version, the cross was made from one third of the beam.

The *Legende* is then a skilful compilation of elements and episodes drawn from many sources. It is a bold and elaborate tale, a fitting culmination of a long process of development. From the early Jewish apocryphal stories of Seth's daring and hopeful mission to the gates of Paradise in quest of mercy, the unknown author led the narrative through the complex maze of symbolic vision, apocryphal episodes linked to Old Testament figures, down to the central point of Christian worship, the redemptive sacrifice of Christ on the Cross. The process of amalgamation was at last completed. It was a strange and complicated process in which pagan and Jewish strands were continually interwoven into the fabric of Christian doctrine. The result was a legend, comparable in scope of design and intricacy of detail to a great tapestry. It was, like the medieval cathedrals, a monument in which pagan, Jewish, and Christian elements were fused by the creative imagination of the faithful.

CONCLUSION

IN EXPLORING the origins of motifs and in tracing the evolution of the legend from its earliest extant beginnings to its culmination in the *Legende,* our study has returned to the point from which it started, the account of the Seth and rood-tree legend which appears in the *Cursor mundi.* It will be found that there is little, if anything, in the *Cursor mundi* version which has not been discussed in this book.

The method of dividing the legends into elements and searching for analogous motifs was considered essential in the analysis of an evolving legend. If this method seems to have disrupted the texts, it is to be regretted, but could not be avoided. The development of the legend is a phenomenon of far greater significance than any particular version and has necessarily been given precedence. In the case of an important work like the *Legende*, we have also tried to consider the text in something like its original entirety.

The vast scope of the subject, ranging from ancient Jewish apocrypha to the literary masterpieces of Calderón, necessitated concentrating on certain aspects of the legend's development. The lack of modern scholarship on the subject suggested that the fullest attention be directed to origins. It was this concentration on the beginnings of the legend which made possible the detection of a number of erroneous assumptions in the work of predecessors. Where the evidence has been sufficient, more tenable proposals have been offered.

Because of the limited scope of this study, much work remains to be done. The legend has been traced only to the point of full development and only the main steps in this development have been outlined. Among the problems which are still relatively unexplored is the whole area of the dispersal of the legend. The *Legende* was copied many times in Latin and translated into almost every known European language. An account of this dispersal in even one of the vernacular languages, with the consequent variations on the basic pattern, would constitute another study. The relationship, too, between medieval iconography and the evolving legend has barely been touched: a systematic investigation might reveal a wealth of relevant data. Indeed, one of the chief purposes of this work is to call the attention of scholars to a relatively new field of research. It is hoped that this study will suggest possibilities which have not been considered before, stimulate more thorough investigations of certain points, and encourage a more extensive study of the whole legend.

We have followed a relatively untrodden path. The influence of Near Eastern concepts on biblical literature has

The Quest of Seth

long been established, and the influence of Near Eastern myths on Jewish apocrypha has recently been worked out; there have also been studies relating ancient apocrypha to medieval literature. But there are few studies which, like the present work, attempt to trace medieval symbols and story patterns not only to Jewish and Christian apocrypha but also to Near Eastern sources.

We have watched the creators of legend, preserving and reinterpreting ancient symbols and ancient stories— symbols and stories deeply rooted in the past, in the belief in animate nature, in animated trees and streams— drawing upon mythological, apocryphal, and folklore traditions, and preserving, but reinterpreting, theologizing to suit an age which had officially, at least, left such primitive beliefs behind, keeping the symbols and stories but imbuing them with new concepts. Some of these ancient images remained unchanged in meaning as well as form; with others the form remained constant, but new ideas were attached to them; with still others a process of change went on—what started out as comparatively simple was elaborated in the course of centuries and became overlaid with theological accretions until in the end both significance and form were materially altered.

We have considered at times, especially in the last chapter, the thorny problem of whether in the case of certain symbols and story patterns we are dealing with the migration of a motif or with its emergence from the "universal unconscious."

We have seen that as a story the Seth legend cannot compete with most medieval narrative. Unlike certain myths and legends which have perennial appeal, for instance the Arthurian cycle, there is nothing of romance and little of adventure of the dragon-slaying, giant-killing variety. As a story, it is not spectacular. Its chief value lies not in its narrative but in its symbolism, in its blend of primordial motifs and theological concepts.

In concluding we might observe that the study of the rood-tree legend provides us with a unique view of the medieval Christian legend-making mind at work, incorporating the apocryphal quest of Seth into its theology, drawing upon dozens of unlikely sources, eliminating and adding, shifting and altering elements, and in the process creating a strange and intricate tale which, like the medieval mystery plays, links the great themes of the Fall and the Redemption.

NOTES

Full bibliographical details for works cited in the notes will be found in the Bibliography.

ABBREVIATIONS

EETS   The Early English Text Society
PG   J. P. Migne, *Patrologia Graeca*
PL   J. P. Migne, *Patrologia Latina*
PMLA   Publications of the Modern Language Association

INTRODUCTION

1. Curtius, *Europäische Literatur und lateinisches Mittelalter.*
2. Halliday, *The Legend of the Rood,* p. 49.
3. Morris (ed.), *Cursor mundi,* EETS, LVII, 78–91; LIX, 367–71, 460 ff., 505–17; LXII, 945–47.
4. *Ibid.,* LXVI-LXVIII-XCIX, 1222 ff.; De Combes, *The Find-*

ing of the Cross, p. 88; Cook (ed.), *The Old English Elene,* pp. xv–xxiv.

5. Cook, *op. cit.*

6. Meyer, "Die Geschichte des Kreuzholzes vor Christus," pp. 162–65.

7. Mandeville, *Travels,* I, 6–7.

8. Caxton, *The Golden Legend,* I, 180; III, 169.

9. Malory, *Works,* II, 990–94. This version, which Meyer, "Die Geschichte," p. 122, placed in Group IV, is different from any other; indeed, it is so different, so brilliant and original that I am preparing a separate study. This form of the legend is also related in *Le saint-graal,* ed. Hucher, I, 452–79; *La queste del saint graal,* ed. Pauphilet, pp. 211–18; and *Grand saint graal,* in *The Vulgate Version of the Arthurian Romances,* ed. Sommer, Vol. I.

10. Gayley, *Plays of Our Forefathers,* pp. 246–71; Meyer, "Die Geschichte," pp. 155, 160.

11. Meyer, "Die Geschichte," p. 152; Norris (ed. and trans.), *Ancient Cornish Drama,* I, 52–67, 131–43, 147–217, and cf. 425–27; see also Halliday (trans.), *The Legend of the Rood.*

12. Morris (ed.), *Legends of the Holy Rood,* pp. 18–46, 19–47, 62–96; Horstmann (ed.), "Canticum de Creatione," pp. 287–331; D'Evelyn and Mill (eds.), *The South English Legendary,* EETS, CCXXXV, 167–74. See also the version in *The Northern Passion,* ed. Foster, EETS, CXLV, 134–67; *The Northern Passion* (Supplement), ed. Heuser and Foster, EETS, CLXXXIII, 31–34, 95–116.

13. Seymour, *The Cross in Tradition, History and Art,* p. 96.

14. Van Marle, *The Development of the Italian Schools of Painting,* III, 539 ff., Figs. 300–302.

15. Longhi, *Piero della Francesca,* Plates XLIII–LXXX.

16. Seymour, p. 96; Ashton, *The Legendary History of the Cross,* pp. lxi–lxxiii, Plate A.

17. Ashton, pp. ci–clxxvi; see also Preface, pp. i–ii. A set of Flemish wood carvings of the sixteenth century, now in the Victoria and Albert Museum, show several episodes of the legend.

18. Mussafia, "Sulla leggenda del legno della Croce," pp. 165–216.

19. Graf, *La leggenda del paradiso terrestre;* an expanded version of this work appeared as "Il Mito del paradiso terrestre," in *Miti, leggende e superstizioni del medio evo,* Vol. I.

20. Meyer, "*Vita Adae et Evae,*" pp. 187–250.

21. Napier (ed.), *History of the Holy Rood-Tree.*

22. Pauphilet, *Étude sur la queste del saint graal,* pp. 145–53.

23. Gayley, pp. 246–71.

24. Rappoport, *Mediaeval Legends of Christ,* pp. 210–34. De Combes gives an account in his appendix, which is based on even earlier sources. The most recent reference to the Seth legend is in Eliade's *Patterns in Comparative Religion,* pp. 292–93.

25. Moses Gaster, *Ilchester Lectures on Greeko-Slavonic Literature*, p. 156.

26. Pauphilet, *Étude*, p. 146.

27. Loomis, *Arthurian Tradition and Chrétien de Troyes*, pp. 38–58.

28. Taylor's classic, *The Medieval Mind*, contains no mention of the legend of Seth and the Holy Cross.

29. Charles (ed.), *The Apocrypha and Pseudepigrapha of the Old Testament*, II, 123–54.

30. Meyer, "Die Geschichte," p. 207.

31. James (trans.), *The Apocryphal New Testament*, pp. 94–128.

32. Meyer, "Die Geschichte," p. 105.

33. *Ibid.*, p. 109.

34. *Ibid.*, p. 112; Meyer, "*Vita Adae et Evae,*" pp. 402–5.

35. According to Meyer, the MSS which contain the interpolated legend of the Cross could not have been made before the end of the twelfth century ("Die Geschichte," p. 108).

36. *Ibid.*, p. 122.

37. *Ibid.*, pp. 117 ff.

38. *Ibid.*, p. 131.

CHAPTER 1

1. Torrey, *The Apocryphal Literature*, pp. 131, 133. Wells (ed.), "The Books of Adam and Eve," in Charles (ed.), *The Apocrypha and Pseudepigrapha of the Old Testament*, II, 123–54; Pfeiffer, *History of New Testament Times*, p. 73; Eissfeldt, *Einleitung in das Alte Testament*, p. 787.

2. Wells, in Charles, II, 124.

3. It has been grouped with pseudepigrapha (falsely attributed to an Old Testament patriarch) to distinguish it from the books known as apocrypha—those present in the Septuagint but not in the Hebrew Bible. See, for instance, the editions of Fabricius, Kautzsch, and Charles. The term pseudepigrapha, however, is now recognized to be outworn and misleading; apocrypha is to be preferred as a general term for extra-canonical literature and hence for *The Apocalypse of Moses* (Torrey, pp. 10–11). On midrash and haggada, see Zeitlin, "Jewish Apocryphal Literature," pp. 248–50; Pfeiffer, "The Literature and Religion of the Pseudepigrapha," p. 425; Torrey, p. 132. "Midrash" is, of course, the more general term; "haggada" is a particular form of midrash.

4. Schürer, *Geschichte des jüdischen Volkes im Zeitalter Jesu Christi*, III, 395; Pfeiffer, *History of New Testament Times*, p. 72.

5. There are six MSS. The earliest of these, D, was edited by Ceriani. Tischendorf in *Apocalypses apocryphae*, pp. 1–23, established a text based on four MSS—A, B, C, and D; a translation of this text appears as *Revelation of Moses* in the "Ante-Nicene Chris-

tian Library," XVI, 454–67. See also the text in *Die Apokryphen und Pseudepigraphen des Alten Testaments,* ed. Kautzsch, II, 506–28, based on later MSS E1 and E2. Our summary is based on the translation of a text derived from MSS C and D in Charles, II, 143–44.

6. Theodor H. Gaster, "The Canaanite Epic of Keret," p. 285.

7. Pritchard (ed.), *Ancient Near Eastern Texts Relating to the Old Testament,* p. 147.

8. Theodor H. Gaster, "The Canaanite Epic of Keret," p. 287.

9. Hooke, "The Myth and Ritual Pattern in Jewish and Christian Apocalyptic," in *The Labyrinth,* pp. 229, 233.

10. Heidel, *The Gilgamesh Epic and Old Testament Parallels,* p. 222, also pp. 268–69.

11. See pp. 27–28, below.

12. Frazer, *The Golden Bough,* III, 1–2.

13. Hooke, *The Labyrinth,* pp. 229–30.

14. Aarne, *Verzeichnis der Märchentypen,* p. 25, translated by Stith Thompson, *The Types of the Folk-Tale,* pp. 89–90. Bolte and Polívka, *Anmerkungen zu den Kinder- und Hausmärchen der Brüder Grimm,* II, 394–401.

15. Brugger, *The Illuminated Tree in Two Arthurian Romances,* pp. 20–21.

16. Meyer, "Die Geschichte," pp. 135–36.

17. *Grimms' Fairy Tales,* pp. 449 ff.

18. Pritchard, *Ancient Near Eastern Texts,* pp. 48, 72, 101.

19. Theodor H. Gaster, *The Oldest Stories in the World,* pp. 48, 51.

20. Kramer, "The Epic of Gilgameš and Its Sumerian Sources," p. 13.

21. Heidel, pp. 8–10, 64–91. On the plant of life see also Widengren, "Mesopotamian Elements in Manichaeism," p. 138; Langdon (ed.), *The Mythology of All Races,* V, 152, 187. Although the plant of life does not appear in *The Apocalypse of Moses,* it is present in later versions of the Seth legend. Cf. Introduction.

22. Pritchard, *Ancient Near Eastern Texts,* pp. 101–2.

23. Langdon, *The Mythology of All Races,* V, 182.

24. Ginzberg, *The Legends of the Jews,* V, 95–96, 163. For Journey to Otherworld with Angel, see Neuman, "Motif-Index of Talmudic-Midrashic Literature," F7; 3 *Baruch* 1:8–17:4, in Charles, II, 533–41; Ginzberg, *Legends of the Jews,* II, 313; Moses Gaster, *The Revelation of Moses, Studies and Texts,* I, 138; 1 *Enoch,* 24–25, in Charles, II, 204–5.

25. For the date of 1 *Enoch* see the following: Torrey, p. 114; Rowley, *The Relevance of Apocalyptic,* pp. 75–80; Charles, II, 170–71.

26. Thompson, *Motif-Index of Folk Literature,* II, 189, lists "Oil of Immortality."

27. Ginzberg, *Legends of the Jews*, I, 93; "Book of Adam," p. 179.

28. Buttenwieser, "Books of Adam," p. 79.

29. Piper observed the word-play in "The Tree of Life," trans. in *Journal of Sacred Literature*, VI (1864), 31; also Wells, in Charles, II, 143 n. and 144 n. See also Theodor H. Gaster, "Myth and Story," pp. 205–6 on the use of word-play.

30. R. S. Loomis and H. W. Wells (trans. and ed.), "St. Nicholas and the Virgins," *Representative Mediaeval and Tudor Plays* (New York, 1942), p. 41; Joseph Q. Adams (ed.), "Everyman," *Chief Pre-Shakespearean Dramas* (New York, 1949), p. 33; *The Faerie Queene*, Bk. I, Canto XI, stanza 48.

31. Theodor H. Gaster, *The Holy and the Profane*, p. 14; see "Oleum" in Pauly-Wissowa, *Real-Encyclopädie der classischen Altertumswissenschaft*, Vol. XVII, cols. 2454–74, esp. 2462.

32. Jastrow, *The Civilization of Babylonia and Assyria*, pp. 252–53; Daiches, *Babylonian Oil Magic*, p. 14.

33. Chase, *Confirmation in the Apostolic Age*, p. 67; Crawley, "Anointing," pp. 549–50.

34. Chase, p. 67.

35. Strong, *The Exhaustive Concordance of the Bible*, pp. 740–41; see also Jastrow, "Anointing (Semitic)," pp. 555–57. For these concepts in apocryphal literature see Charles, II, 309, 443.

36. All biblical references are to the Douay version, unless otherwise indicated.

37. Charles, II, 143.

38. Widengren, "The King and the Tree of Life in Ancient Near Eastern Religion," pp. 59–60.

39. Charles, II, 126; according to Pfeiffer, "The Literature and Religion of the Pseudepigrapha," p. 435, *2 Enoch* belongs to the first half of the first century A.D.

40. *2 Enoch* 8:3–5, in Charles, II, 434; Charles, II, 143 n.; Ginzberg, *Legends of the Jews*, V, 119 n. 113.

41. In the belief of the ancient Egyptians, Babylonians, and Assyrians, the tree of life was a date palm; Hooke (ed.), *Myth and Ritual*, pp. 141–42; Langdon, pp. 117, 179. Similarly in the Jewish apocalypse, *1 Enoch* 24:3–5, in Charles, II, 204.

42. Ginzberg, *Legends of the Jews*, V, 119 n. 113.

43. "Ante-Nicene Fathers," IV, 585; Ginzberg, *Legends of the Jews*, V, 119 n. 113; cf. also Scott, "Ophitism," p. 500.

44. "Ante-Nicene Fathers," VIII, 89. Rylands, *The Beginnings of Gnostic Christianity*, p. 137.

45. *4 Ezra* 7:123, in Charles, II, 591. For the healing powers of the tree of life in Mesopotamian ritual and myth, see Widengren, "Mesopotamian Elements," p. 155.

46. Ginzberg, *Legends of the Jews*, V, 119 n. 113, 11 n. 22; Patai, *Man and Temple*, p. 207.

47. Ginzberg, *Legends of the Jews*, I, 10, 334, 354; III, 95; IV, 197, 333, 360, etc.

48. Isa. 26:19.

49. *2 Baruch* chaps. 29–30, 73, in Charles, II, 498, 518.

50. Charles, II, 433, 443.

51. See n. 29 above.

52. *Apocalypsis Mosis* 28, in Charles, II, 148.

53. *1 Enoch* 25, in Charles, II, 204–5.

54. *Testament of Levi* 18:10–11, in Charles, II, 315. Although the present Greek text of the *Testament of Levi* is, according to De Jonge, *The Testaments of the Twelve Patriarchs*, p. 52, relatively late, it is based on an older Jewish source. Rowley, *Jewish Apocalyptic and the Dead Sea Scrolls*, p. 13, reports that some fragments of a *Testament of Levi* have been found among the Dead Sea Scrolls.

55. *Apocalypsis Mosis* 3, in Charles, II, 139.

56. *Apocalypsis Mosis* 22, *ibid.*, p. 147.

57. See n. 53 above.

58. *1 Enoch* 40:9 and 71:3, in Charles, II, 211, 236.

59. *3 Baruch* 15:1–2, in Charles, II, 540–41. Torrey, p. 126, dates *3 Baruch* before A.D. 70. Cf. *2 Enoch* 22:8, in Charles, II, 443.

60. Kohler, "The Essenes and the Apocalyptic Literature," p. 163.

61. Burkitt, *Jewish and Christian Apocalypses*, p. 42, relates the belief that the righteous will be rewarded in the world to come with the destruction of Jerusalem. See also Frost, *Old Testament Apocalyptic*, p. 18.

62. Rappoport, *Myth and Legend of Ancient Israel*, I, 199–203.

63. James, *The Lost Apocrypha of the Old Testament*, p. 9. Cf. Ginzberg, *Legends of the Jews*, V, 149.

64. Charles, II, 167, 170, 172; Torrey, p. 114; Rowley, pp. 52, 75 ff.; Eissfeldt, p. 765.

65. *1 Enoch* 24–25, in Charles, II, 204–5; cf. p. 28.

66. Gayley, p. 267.

67. James, *The Lost Apocrypha*, p. 9; Ginzberg, *Legends of the Jews*, V, 149; Georgius Syncellus, *Chronographia*, pp. 16–17.

68. James, p. 9.

69. Ginzberg, *Legends of the Jews*, V, 158 n. 59, 126 n. 137.

70. On fusion of character see Loomis, *Arthurian Tradition and Chrétien de Troyes*, pp. 50–51.

71. See, for example, Rylaarsdam, "Intertestamental Studies since Charles' Apocrypha and Pseudepigrapha," pp. 32–51.

72. Meyer, "Vita Adae et Evae," pp. 207, 209; Charles, II, 129. There are 24 known MSS of the Latin *Vita;* 12 of them were used by Meyer in the preparation of his text. He divided these 12 MSS into 4 classes: Class I represents the earliest form; there are 3 MSS of this class, all from Munich, dated 9th, 10th, and 12th centuries. Class II, represented by 4 Munich MSS, dated 13th, 14th, and 15th centuries, contains 2 interpolations, which are not, however, rele-

vant to this study. Class III, represented by 4 Munich MSS of the 15th century, will be considered at some length later since it contains interpolations from the rood-tree legend. Meyer's Class IV is represented by a Paris MS of the 9th century which belongs essentially to Class II. In addition to these 12 MSS, from which Meyer derived his text, there are 12 MSS in England, dated 13th to 15th centuries, which Mozley used as the basis of his text. Of these Mozley assigned 11 to Meyer's Class II; 1 to Class III; the latter MS contains a fully developed form of the Seth and rood-tree legend and will be considered in chap. 5 (Mozley, "The *Vita Adae*," pp. 121 ff.).

73. In Charles, II, 124, 125.
74. Meyer, "*Vita Adae et Evae*," p. 207.
75. *Ibid.*, pp. 198, 207.
76. Charles, II, 128–29.
77. *Ibid.*, p. 134.
78. *Ibid.*, p. 141. One point on which the two differ—the interpolation from *The Gospel of Nicodemus* in the *Vita*—will be considered in chap. 2. It appears in Section XLII of both Meyer's text and Charles's translation, but both agree it was made at a later date (Meyer, "*Vita Adae et Evae*," pp. 202–3; Charles, II, 126, 128, 129, 144).
79. Charles, II, 148.
80. *Ibid.*, p. 145.

CHAPTER 2

1. Hulme (ed.), *The Middle English Harrowing of Hell and Gospel of Nicodemus*, p. lxiv. The title, *Evangelium Nicodemi*, seems not to have appeared before the thirteenth century; see MacCulloch, *The Harrowing of Hell*, p. 153, and Tischendorf (ed.), *Evangelia Apocrypha*, p. lix.
2. Hulme, *The Middle English Harrowing of Hell*, p. lx; MacCulloch, p. 153; James, *The Apocryphal New Testament*, p. 117.
3. Tischendorf, *Evangelia Apocrypha*, p. lxvii; Hulme, *The Middle English Harrowing of Hell*, p. lxi; MacCulloch, pp. 155–56.
4. Lipsius, "Gospels Apocryphal," p. 709; Hulme, *The Middle English Harrowing of Hell*, p. lxii; Von Dobschütz, "Gospel of Nicodemus," p. 545.
5. Cf. Introduction.
6. Tischendorf, *Evangelia Apocrypha*, p. lxvii.
7. See, for instance, Lipsius, "Gospels Apocryphal," p. 709; Maury, *Croyances et légendes de l'antiquité*, p. 294; Hulme, *The Middle English Harrowing of Hell*, p. lxi; Hulme, "The Old English Version of the Gospel of Nicodemus," p. 459.
8. Lipsius, "Gospels Apocryphal," p. 709.
9. Von Dobschütz, p. 546.

10. MacCulloch, *The Harrowing of Hell*, p. 158.

11. Von Dobschütz was to have investigated this point—as well as many another unresolved problem—in his new critical edition of the *Descensus*, but it seems to have been incomplete at the time of his death in 1934 (Von Dobschütz, p. 545; James, *The Apocryphal New Testament*, p. 94).

12. Hulme, *The Middle English Harrowing of Hell*, p. lxii; MacCulloch, pp. 1–10, 320–23.

13. MacCulloch, pp. 283–86, 312–19; Hulme, *The Middle English Harrowing of Hell*, p. lxii. Ginzberg, *Legends of the Jews*, V, 413 n. 118, gives Hebrew sources.

14. MacCulloch, pp. 45–66; Hulme, *The Middle English Harrowing of Hell*, p. lxii. I Pet. 3:19, 4:6; Acts 2:24, 31; Rom. 10:7, Matt. 27:52, 53.

15. Hulme, *The Middle English Harrowing of Hell*, p. lxiii; Maury, pp. 313 ff.; Nicolas, *Études sur les évangiles apocryphes*, p. 303.

16. Hulme, *The Middle English Harrowing of Hell*, p. lxiii; McGiffert, *The Apostles' Creed*, p. 191.

17. MacCulloch, p. 171.

18. According to von Dobschütz, the best edition of the *Descensus* is Thilo's, but Tischendorf's has been more widely used. Tischendorf established a Greek text based on three MSS (pp. 301–11) and two Latin texts: A, based on four MSS (pp. 368–95), and B, based on three MSS (pp. 396–410). These three texts have been translated by James in *The Apocryphal New Testament*, and these are the translations which will be used in our analysis.

19. James, *The Apocryphal New Testament*, pp. 126–27.

20. On typology, see Goppelt, *Typos. Die typologische Deutung des Alten Testaments im Neuen;* Lundberg, *La typologie baptismale dans l'ancienne église;* Lampe and Woollcombe, *Essays on Typology*. The typological relationship in the *Descensus*, however, is between Old Testament apocryphal material and New Testament apocryphal material. To my knowledge, this area has not been explored.

21. II Pet. 3:8; Ps. 89:4.

22. MacCulloch, p. 332; *Epistle of Barnabas*, p. 127; Irenaeus, *Against Heresies*, p. 557; Julius Africanus, *Chronography*, p. 138; Frost, *Old Testament Apocalyptic*, p. 20, has traced the figure 6,000 to Zoroastrianism.

23. Purification ceremonies are exceedingly ancient. Christian baptism, however, was instituted to wipe out original sin. In the *Descensus* the baptism of Adam, coming as it must after death, wiped away not only original sin, but actual sin and thus made possible his restoration to Paradise. The practice of baptizing at the hour of death or even after death was not uncommon in the early centuries, especially among the Gnostic sects. Widengren, "Mesopotamian Elements in Manichaeism," pp. 108, 121, traces the prac-

tice to ancient Babylonian purificatory rites. See also MacCulloch, pp. 133, 246, 248.

24. Bernard, "The Descent into Hades and Christian Baptism," p. 9; I Pet. 3:19; Rom. 6:3.

25. Bernard, "The Descent," pp. 15, 23, 24; Bernard (ed.), *The Odes of Solomon; The Pastor of Hermas*, p. 49; *The Epistle of the Apostles*, in James, *The Apocryphal New Testament*, p. 494.

26. Bernard, "The Descent," pp. 30, 33, 37.

27. *Ibid.*, pp. 1–9; Bernard, *The Odes of Solomon*, Introduction, p. 32.

28. I have used the translations of Cumont, "La cosmogonie manichéene d'après Théodore bar Khôni," pp. 46–48; Burkitt, *The Religion of the Manichees*, pp. 14, 31; Widengren, "Mesopotamian Elements in Manichaeism," p. 123; for the interpretation of Christ's baptizing Adam, I am indebted to Widengren.

29. James, *The Apocryphal New Testament*, p. 49.

30. Matt. 3:6, 3:13–16; Mark 1:5, 1:9.

31. The Manichaean *Acts of Thomas* (Greek, third century) provides an interesting parallel to the anointing with the oil of mercy in connection with baptism. Here at the baptism of Iuzanes, the Apostle Thomas took oil and spoke thus: "Let his [Christ's] victorious might come and be established in this oil, like as it was established in the tree that was its kin." Then followed the pouring of the oil. Here then is probably a reference to the oil of the tree of life used in baptism (James, pp. 228, 364, 418, 433). See also Lake, "Baptism," pp. 388–89. Cf. chap. 1, for use of oil from the tree of life in the initiation ceremonies of the Ophites and for Christ's anointing with oil from the tree of life in the Gnostic *Recognitions of Clement*.

32. MacCulloch, p. 332.

33. Tertullian, *On Baptism*, p. 672.

34. Lake, p. 389. Cf. the ancient custom of anointing the body after bathing.

35. Tertullian, p. 672. In the baptisms described by Cyril of Jerusalem (*ca.* 340), the anointing both precedes and follows immersion. Cross (ed.), *St. Cyril of Jerusalem's Lectures on the Sacraments*, pp. 60–65.

36. Cumont, "La cosmogonie manichéene," pp. 46–49; Burkitt, *The Religion of the Manichees*, p. 31; Widengren, "Mesopotamian Elements," p. 123.

37. Bernard pointed out that in the Eastern Fathers, especially Origen, Gregory of Nyssa, Cyril, and Basil, the relationship is often established between baptism as a release from bondage and as a restoration to Paradise (*Odes of Solomon*, pp. 34, 74; "The Descent," p. 13).

38. There were many versions of the *Descensus* in which the Seth legend was recognized as extraneous and therefore omitted.

39. Hulme, *The Middle English Harrowing of Hell*, p. lxiv. For

The Gospel of Nicodemus in Spanish, French, German, etc., see Wülcker, *Das Evangelium Nicodemi in der abendländischen Literatur;* in Ireland see Crotty, "The Exeter 'Harrowing of Hell': A Re-Interpretation," p. 349.

40. Hulme, *The Middle English Horrowing of Hell,* p. lxvii.

41. Chap. 19 of *The Gospel of Nicodemus* at chap. 42 of the *Vita.* Meyer, "*Vita Adae et Evae,*" pp. 202–3, 235–36; Charles, II, 126, 128, 144.

CHAPTER 3

1. From Constantine's vision stems a related tradition: the exaltation of the form of the cross. In sculpture and poetry the cross triumphant appears, carved and jeweled. See for instance, the Ruthwell and Bewcastle crosses and the "Dream of the Rood." In this poem, as in the rood-tree legends, the cross is personified and endowed with dignity and a sense of its unique destiny.

2. Napier, *History of the Holy Rood-Tree,* pp. 2–35. A. G. Brunner was listed in *PMLA,* April, 1952, p. 144, as being in the process of preparing an edition of MS Bodleian 343, but this edition has evidently not been completed.

3. Napier, p. xii.

4. Napier, p. lviii; Ker, "An Eleventh Century Old English Legend of the Cross before Christ," pp. 84–85.

5. Meyer, "Die Geschichte," p. 106.

6. Napier, pp. 2–35.

7. Meyer, "Die Geschichte," p. 156; Napier, pp. xxxv–xlii; cf. Introduction and chap. 6.

8. Napier, pp. xiv, xxxv, xli, xliii, xliv–xlvi.

9. Mussafia, "Sulla leggenda del paradiso terrestre," pp. 165–79; Meyer, "Die Geschichte," 106; Jacoby, "Kreuzbaum, Kreuzholz," col. 488.

10. Moses Gaster, *Ilchester Lectures.*

11. *Ibid.,* pp. 23, 25, 29, 35–37. See also Wesselofsky, "Altslavische Kreuz- und Rebensagen," pp. 134–37.

12. Cf. Jewish legends and later rood-tree legends in which Moses' rod is represented as coming from Paradise. Ginzberg, *Legends of the Jews,* III, 477; VI, 14.

13. A tree with tripartite structure of the trunk appears on a frieze of ivory, found at Assur. According to van Buren, *Symbols of the Gods in Mesopotamian Art,* p. 27, the tripartite structure was an essential feature of the severely formalized sacred tree of the first millennium.

14. Meyer, "Die Geschichte," p. 106; Moses Gaster, *Ilchester Lectures,* p. 156, believed Meyer's failure to consider Slavonic versions marred his otherwise useful study.

15. Gaster, *Ilchester Lectures*, pp. 19, 148–51, 155; see also James, *Apocrypha anecdota*, pp. 156–57.

16. Gaster, *Ilchester Lectures*, pp. 195–99, refers to the Albigensian schools where in 1025 a vernacular Bible was studied and assumes that this Bible contained legendary and heretical material similar to that of the Bogomils.

17. Runciman, *The Medieval Manichee*, pp. 81–86, 167–68; Obolensky, *The Bogomils*, pp. 271–74, 281–82. The whole subject of the relationship between Eastern and Western versions of rood-tree legends needs a more thorough investigation than is possible here; it should preferably be undertaken by someone who, like Gaster, knows not only West European and Slavonic languages, but also Hebrew.

18. Gaster, *Ilchester Lectures*, pp. 151–82, 195–99. A similar version in Slavonic, already separated from its heretical origins, is cited by Kozak, "Bibliographische Übersicht der biblisch-apokryphen Literatur bei den Slaven," p. 140, entitled "Historia de ligno crucis."

19. Mussafia, p. 179; Meyer, "Die Geschichte," p. 156; Gretser, *De sancta cruce, Opera omnia* II, 429.

20. Smith, "Notes on 'The Assyrian Tree,'" p. 72. Cf. Jeremias 10:3–4.

21. Napier, p. xi.

22. Lengthening and shortening is a common folklore motif. See C. Grant Loomis, *White Magic*, p. 89; Chambers, *Arthur of Britain*, pp. 7, 240; Holmberg, *Mythology of All Races*, IV (Siberian), 353–54; Ginzberg, *On Jewish Law and Lore*, pp. 88–89; Ginzberg, *Legends of the Jews*, VI, 67 n. 344. For a Jewish tradition of the wood which changed its size in connection with Solomon's building the Temple, see Seligsohn, "Solomon," p. 441.

23. For the tree which cannot be moved see Gregory of Tours, *De gloria martyrum, PL,* Vol. LXXI, cols. 713 ff. For the tree which can be cut down only by a destined hero, see Kramer, "The Epic of Gilgameš and Its Sumerian Sources," pp. 19–20.

24. De Combes, *The Finding of the Cross*, p. 264; Cook (ed.), *The Old English Elene*, pp. xx–xxii; Gradon (ed.), *Cynewulf's Elene*, p. 15.

25. A very old feature of the legend. See Cook (ed.), *The Old English Elene*, pp. xx–xxi.

26. See Ginzberg, *Legends of the Jews*, VI, 106–7, for references to Jewish legends in which the rod was passed from Moses to David and was intended to be used in the time of the Messiah.

27. This attributing a knowledge of the Trinity to Moses is not peculiar to legend, as one may discover from reading the early Greek Fathers. See especially Justin Martyr's *First Apology*, p. 183, and Anastasius Sinaita, *De trinitate*, p. 441. See also Ames, "The Debate between the Church and the Synagogue," pp. 7, 9, 21, for the way ideas of this sort developed from controversies between Christians and Jews.

28. Isa. 60:13 in Septuagint, not Vulgate as Seymour stated.

29. Justin Martyr, *First Apology*, p. 173; Tertullian, *An Answer to the Jews*, p. 166; *Against Marcion*, p. 337; Irenaeus, *Against Heresies*, p. 545.

30. Darnedde, *Deutsche Sibyllen-Weissagung*, pp. 10–17.

31. Kinter, "Prophetess and Fay: A Study of the Ancient and Medieval Tradition of the Sibyl," p. 49. According to Kinter, "sensuality is important in . . . the Sibylla-Apollo stories." For the relationship between sensuality and prophecy he refers the reader to Silvio Ferri, *La Sibilla. Saggio sulla religione popolare Greca* (Pisa, 1915), p. 100 and *passim*.

32. Lactantius, *Epitome of the Divine Institutes*, Bk. I, chap. 5.

33. Lanchester, "Sibylline Oracles," p. 497. See also Darnedde, pp. 17–19.

34. Lanchester, p. 498, and Darnedde, pp. 20–24.

35. Lanchester, p. 499.

36. Kurfess (ed. and trans.), *Sibyllinische Weissagungen*, pp. 150, 151. As indications of the currency of this prophecy see Sozomenus, *Ecclesiastical History*, Bk. I, chap. 1, and Bk. II, chap. 1. Cassiodorus, *Historia tripartita*, *PL*, Vol. LXIX, col. 927; Andreas Cretensis, *In exaltationem s. crucis. I*, *PG*, Vol. XCVII, col. 1027; Hertz, "Die Rätsel der Königin von Saba," p. 22.

37. Pausanias, *Description of Greece*, IV, 431 ff.

38. Herr, "La reine de Saba et le bois de la croix," pp. 18–19; Georgius Monachus, *Chronicon*, *PG*, Vol. CX, cols. 251 ff.; Hertz, pp. 19–20.

39. This merging of queen and sibyl in an early Greek source fits in very well with our theory that the original version of the rood-tree legend was in Greek. See also the later Greek writers, Georgius Cedrenus (eleventh century), *PG*, Vol. CXXI, col. 200, and Michael Glycas (twelfth century), *PG*, Vol. CLVIII, col. 352. Hertz, p. 23, and Herr, p. 20. As we shall observe later, sibylline oracles from the Eighth Book were placed in the mouth of the Queen of Sheba.

40. Dan. 13. Very popular in the twelfth to fourteenth centuries, the story was probably also well known in the eleventh. Mozley, "Susanna and the Elders: Three Medieval Poems," pp. 27 ff.

41. Mandeville in his *Travels*, p. 45, relates the story of a maiden, accused of fornication and condemned to be burned; as the flames mounted, she prayed, and the fire was quenched.

42. See Meyer, "Die Geschichte," p. 106, for an account of the MSS, pp. 106–7 for the text.

43. It would seem that not only is Zöckler mistaken, as Meyer stated, but that Meyer himself is mistaken concerning the origin of the tree with the three kinds of leaves. Meyer, "Die Geschichte," p. 107; Zöckler, *Das Kreuz Christi*, pp. 469–70.

44. Mâle, *L'art religieux du XIIᵉ siècle en France*, p. 396; Rabanus Maurus, *Commentaria in Libros II Paralipomenon*, *PL*, Vol. CIX, cols. 472–73.

45. There is also in Solomon's action the well-known folklore pattern of the futile attempt to avoid an unwelcome fate which has been prophesied. See Stith Thompson, Vol. V, M 370.

46. This passage, John 5:2, is an excellent example of the tendency to reinterpret traditional material in terms of the prevailing concepts of the age: Howard, in commenting on this passage, stated that recent excavations have disclosed a pool bearing votive inscriptions which suggest that ancient superstition ascribed healing virtue to the water. "The disturbance of the water caused by an intermittent spring was in primitive times attributed to the action of a local divinity. Jewish superstition substituted an angel" (*The Interpreter's Bible*, VIII, 539–40). The rationalizing medieval legend-maker provided the angel with a motive for stirring the water—the search for the holy wood!

47. As Meyer pointed out, elements of the legend at approximately this stage of development appear in a number of writers of the twelfth and thirteenth centuries: Honorius of Autun in *Speculum ecclesiae* (before 1125), *PL*, Vol. CLXXII, col. 994; Petrus Comestor in *Historia scholastica* (before 1178), *PL*, Vol. CXCVIII, cols. 1369 and 1578. Meyer, "Die Geschichte," pp. 108–9. In the passage in Honorius of Autun's *Speculum ecclesiae* a more appropriate motive has been assigned the angel who stirred the waters of the Probatica Pool: it was out of reverence for the wood. In both passages in Petrus Comestor the wood was buried deep in the earth and later, on this spot, the pool sprang up. According to Meyer, the first passage in Comestor was copied by Vincent of Beauvais in his *Speculum historiale* and by Petrus de Riga in *Aurora;* the second passage in Comestor appears in the *Otia imperialia* of Gervasius of Tilbury; both passages in Comestor were used by Jacobus de Voragine, who was in turn the source for many later versions. The appearance of the legend in these works is significant in the transmission rather than in the evolution of the legend.

CHAPTER 4

1. Meyer, "Die Geschichte," pp. 112–14.

2. *Ibid.,* p. 109.

3. It is to be noted that these are not the same three woods mentioned in the Bodleian MS 343. Both the Bodleian version and Geoffrey mention cypress, but whereas the Bodleian adds cedar and pine, Geoffrey mentions fir and palm. The palm, traditional symbol of life, victory, and resurrection, and one of the trees used by Solomon in the construction of his Temple, was often cited as one of the three or four woods of which the cross was believed to have been made (Goblet d'Alviella, *The Migration of Symbols,* pp. 145, 151; Ferguson, *Signs and Symbols in Christian Art,* p. 45; Mackay, "The Sign of the Palm Tree," pp. 187–212). The fir was mentioned

less frequently; it, too, was used by Solomon in the construction of the Temple (III Kings 5:8, 15; 6:34).

4. Cf. Graf, *Miti*, p. 81, and Meyer, "Die Geschichte," p. 112: "Dieser Athanasius ist nicht zu bestimmen."

5. Meyer, "Die Geschichte," p. 161.

6. Sackur, *Sibyllinische Texte und Forschungen*, pp. 8–9. Sackur edited the prophecies from four Latin MSS of the eighth century.

7. Ogle, "Petrus Comestor, Methodius, and the Saracens," p. 318.

8. Sackur noted his appearance in the Syriac work of the sixth century, *The Cave of Treasures*, where he is called Jonton. Sackur, pp. 10–11, 14, 54; Bezold (ed. and trans.), *Die Schatzhöhle*, p. 33. Cf. Moses Gaster, *The Chronicles of Jerahmeel*, pp. 69–70, Introduction, p. li.

9. Sackur, pp. 14–15, 63. Also see Kayser (trans.), *Das Buch von der Erkenntniss der Wahrheit*, p. 259. For Seth as an astronomer, see Ginzberg, *Legends of the Jews*, I, 121; V, 149 n. 53.

10. Ginzberg, *Legends of the Jews*, II, 291, 293; V, 105; VI, 66.

11. Moses Gaster, *The Chronicles of Jerahmeel*, pp. 36–37; Jagić, "Slavische Beiträge zu den biblischen Apocryphen," pp. 24–25, 88.

12. Baring-Gould, *Curious Myths of the Middle Ages*, p. 379.

13. Josephus, *Jewish Antiquities*, pp. 657, 661; Herodotus, I, 387–89; see also Ewald, *Geschichte des Volkes Israel*, III, 362, and Hertz, "Die Rätsel der Königen von Saba," p. 25. For Nicaula in plastic art see Molsdorf, *Führer durch den symbolischen und typologischen Bilderkreis der Christlichen Kunst des Mittelalters*, pp. 91–92.

14. For instance, Solomon attempts to avoid the fulfilment of the Queen's prophecy by sinking the wood in the pool of Siloe. Later the pool of Siloe is identified with the Probatica Pool, a natural identification of the two pools in Jerusalem where the afflicted were healed (Siloe–John 9:7).

15. Meyer, "Die Geschichte," p. 109. The interpolation appears at the beginning of the third book in the Windberger MS and in one other MS which Meyer dates the end of the twelfth century. Cf. *PL*, Vol. CLXXII, col. 165. See Meyer, "Die Geschichte," pp. 110–11 for the complete text.

16. Meyer, "Die Geschichte," p. 111.

17. I Cor. 15:21–22. Cf. Rom. 5:12 ff.

18. Irenaeus, *Against Heresies*, p. 545. This general relationship between the first and second Adam is stressed in the Ethiopian *Book of Adam and Eve*, ed. and trans. Malan, pp. 114–15. See also *The Gospel of Nicodemus*, in James, *The Apocryphal New Testament*, p. 137.

19. Jameson, *History of Our Lord*, II, 207; Zöckler, *Das Kreuz Christi*, p. 468; Piper, "Adams Grab auf Golgatha," p. 19; Ginzberg, *Legends of the Jews*, V, 125–26 n. 137; Albright, "The Location of the Garden of Eden," p. 28 n. 1.

20. Piper, "Adams Grab," p. 19.

21. Origen, *Commentariorum series*, XI, 265.

22. Athanasius (Dubia), *De passione et cruce domini*, PG, Vol. XXVIII, cols. 206–7; Basil, *Enarratio in prophetam Isaiam*, chap. 5, PG, Vol. XXX; Chrysostom, *Commentarius in sanctum Joannem. Homilia LXXXV*, PG, Vol. LIX, col. 459; Epiphanius, *Adversus haereses*, Bk. XLVI, chap. 5. Piper, p. 22; also Zöckler, pp. 234–35.

23. Ambrose, *Letters*, p. 244. *Expositionis in Lucam*, PL, Vol. XV, col. 1925.

24. Jerome, *Letters and Select Works*, p. 61. There are many art representations of this motif; see, for instance, Jameson, II, 207–8; Piper, pp. 25–29; Jung, *Symbols of Transformation*, Plate XXXVII.

25. Ginzberg, *Legends of the Jews*, V, 125–26 n. 137.

26. Gen. 23:2.

27. Jerome, *Liber Josue*, p. 386; *In Matth. 27:33*, p. 232; *De situ et nominibus locorum Hebraicorum*, PL, Vol. XXIII, col. 906.

28. Piper, p. 22. Cf. Zöckler, pp. 234–35.

29. The moving of Adam's corpse also occurs in the Ethiopian *Book of Adam and Eve*, but it is there more logically presented: Adam's body, removed from Hebron at the time of the Flood and placed on the ark, was later buried at Golgotha.

30. Ginzberg, *Legends of the Jews*, I, 100.

31. *The Apocalypse of Moses* 40:1–2 in Charles, II, 151.

32. *Vita Adae et Evae* 48:4–5; in Charles, II, 151.

33. Malan (ed. and trans.), *The Book of Adam and Eve*, Preface, p. v.

34. Ginzberg, *Legends of the Jews*, V, 98 n. 70; VI, 14 n. 82.

35. Tertullian, *An Answer to the Jews*, p. 170; Julius Firmicus Maternus, *De errore profanarum religionum*, PL, Vol. XII, cols. 1037–38; Augustine, *Sermo I*, chap. 4; *Sermo LXXXIV*, chap. 3, PL, Vol. XXXIX.

36. Zöckler, pp. 469–70; Anastasius Sinaitica, *Anagogicarum contemplationum in hexaemeron*, PG, Vol. LXXXIX, cols. 944–45.

37. Koberstein, "Uber die in Sage und Dichtung gangbare Vorstellung von dem Fortleben abgeschiedener menschlicher Seelen in der Pflanzenwelt," pp. 73–100. MacCulloch, *The Childhood of Fiction*, p. 115 n. 4. Perhaps the best known example is in the romance of Tristam and Iseult, Koberstein, p. 85. See also Stith Thompson, I, 330.

38. Koberstein, pp. 87 and 89.

39. Isa. 11:4.

40. Isa. 11:1, 10; Rohault de Fleury, *La Sainte Vierge*, I, 17–19; Mâle, *L'art religieux du XIIᵉ siècle en France*, pp. 145, 170, 173; Mâle, *Religious Art in France in the Thirteenth Century*, p. 165 n. 4; Watson, *The Early Iconography of the Tree of Jesse*, pp. 52–54, 87.

41. L'abbé J. Corblet, "Étude iconographique sur l'arbre de Jesse," p. 55.

42. Didron, *Manuel d'iconographie chrétienne grecque et latine,* p. 154 n. 1.

43. Grimm, *Teutonic Mythology,* I, 280–81; IV, 1371.

44. Simrock, *Handbuch der deutschen Mythologie,* pp. 391–93; cf. Mâle, *L'art religieux du XIIe siècle en France,* pp. 394–97; Holmes, *Adenet le Rois' Berte aus grans piés,* p. 11.

45. See also Mannhardt, *Germanische Mythen,* p. 651 n. 1, for reference to Saba as one of the three norns. Cf. the reference to Sibe and Sabie in Haupt, *Untersuchungen zur deutschen Saga,* I, 43.

46. Grimm, *Teutonic Mythology,* I, 272.

47. *Ibid.,* p. 429.

48. M. Gaster, "Zur Quellenkunde deutscher Sagen und Märchen," p. 292; Cassel, *Das Buch Esther,* p. 249. Emil Hirsch dates it *ca.* 800, *Jewish Encyclopedia,* V, 234; Rösch, 9th–10th centuries, "Die Königin von Saba als Königin Bilqîs," p. 546; Hertz, 12th century, "Die Rätsel der Königin von Saba," pp. 4–5.

49. Maulānā Muhammad 'Ali, *The Holy Qur'ān,* Pt. XIX, chap. 27:44. According to Berlinger, "Legenden," col. 107, the intermediary in the transference of the legend from Hebrew to Arabic was Vahab Ibn Munabbih, a Jew who was converted to Islam *ca.* 728.

50. Hertz, p. 6; Berlinger, col. 107.

51. See also Littmann, "The Legend of the Queen of Sheba in the Tradition of Axum," p. 28.

52. There are other versions in which she is reputed to have either hair on her feet or ass's feet but does not (Hammer-Purgstall, *Rosenöl,* I, 162; Weil, *Biblische Legenden der Muselmänner,* p. 237). In one Arabic text the Queen has a goat's foot (Budge, *The Queen of Sheba and Her Only Son Menyelek,* p. xlvii; Bezold, "Kebra Nagast. Die Herrlichkeit der Könige").

53. According to Hertz, p. 14, the meeting of Balqîs and Solomon remains a favorite subject for plastic art representation in the Orient.

54. Hertz, pp. 23–24.

55. The cross is referred to as a bridge in a hymn of Ephraim Syrus (4th century), but it is unlikely that this metaphor could account for the motif of the wood's being used as a bridge in our legend (*Homily on Our Lord,* p. 305; MacCulloch, *The Harrowing of Hell,* p. 115).

56. See Budge, p. xlvii, for an Arabic version in which the Queen's goat foot touches the wood and is transformed.

57. Menner (ed.), *The Poetical Dialogues of Solomon and Saturn,* pp. 5, 22, 23, 47, mentions the following sources: Augustine, *Enarratio in Psalmum,* 126, *PL,* Vol. XXXVII, col. 1688; Isidore, *Allegoriae, PL,* Vol. LXXXIII, col. 113; Ambrose, *PL,* Vol. XV, col. 1585; *Greek Testament of Solomon* (3d–4th centuries).

58. Hertz, p. 25.

59. Berlinger, col. 107.

60. Moses Gaster, "Zur Quellenkunde deutscher Sagen und Märchen," pp. 293, 294; *Acta sanctorum,* Feb. III, 228.

61. Also Ginzberg, *Legends of the Jews,* IV, 143–44. Maulānā Muhammad 'Ali, *The Holy Qur'ān,* Pt. XIX, chap. 27:28.

62. *The Oration in Praise of Constantine,* pp. 574–75, appended by Eusebius to his *Life of Constantine. The City of God,* Bk. XVIII, chap. 23.

63. Kurfess (ed. and trans.), *Sibyllinische Weissagungen,* pp. 170–71 ff. For these lines in Latin mystery plays see Du Méril, *Les origines latines du théatre moderne,* pp. 185–86, 189–90.

64. Hertz (p. 23) connects him with Markolf. In the 14th-century German romance, *Salman und Morolf,* he is Solomon's brother (Menner, p. 27); in Russian tales Solomon's brother is Kitovras (*ibid.,* p. 25). See also Duff (ed.), *The Dialogue between the Wise King Salomon and Marcolphus,* p. 3, where we are told that Marcolf was of short stature.

CHAPTER 5

1. Meyer, "Die Geschichte," p. 116.

2. According to Meyer, four big additions at the end of sections 42, 43, 44, and 48 (Meyer, *"Vita Adae et Evae,"* p. 215; Charles, II, 145). There are also a number of Latin MSS of the *Vita* in England; see Mozley, "The *Vita Adae,"* pp. 121–49. The one MS which Mozley cited as belonging to Class III (Balliol 228) and the only one of the Class II MSS to contain rood-tree material (Arundel 326) both seem to have been influenced by the *Legende,* especially the Balliol. The other English MSS of the *Vita* are not relevant to our purpose.

3. Meyer, *"Vita Adae et Evae,"* pp. 236–42.

4. That trees are embodiments of the life spirit is one of the oldest and most universal of man's beliefs (Frazer, II, 7–58). On the ritual plucking of a bough, see also T. H. Gaster (ed.), *The New Golden Bough,* p. xxiii.

5. The practical use of oil—for food, adornment, and medicine—probably preceded its ritual use, but the point, which cannot be settled here, is not essential to our thesis.

6. The bough (often with three leaves) was used in ancient Mesopotamian ceremonies to banish illness (Widengren, "The King and the Tree of Life," pp. 24–26; Van Buren, *The Flowing Vase and the God with Streams,* pp. 40, 54). Evidence of the use of branches in healing rituals is present, too, in Jewish sources. According to Patai, "The Jerusalem Talmud records that . . . branches were waved over sick persons as a remedy" (*Man and Temple,* p. 38).

7. Widengren ("The King and the Tree of Life," pp. 20 ff.), demonstrates how pervasive was the use of the twig of the tree of life in the rituals of the divine kings of Mesopotamia.

8. Van Buren, p. 78, also pp. 61, 65, 77, 127, 129.

9. *Ibid.,* pp. 13–14.

10. Homer *The Odyssey* xi; Rahner, *Griechische Mythen in christlicher Deutung,* pp. 232 ff., see also pp. 361 ff.

11. Goblet d'Alviella, p. 227.

12. Frazer, II, 293–95. From the *Aeneid* vi, we know the magic branch as the golden bough with which Aeneas descends into the underworld.

13. See also Stith Thompson, II, 111–14.

14. Ginzberg, V, 149; James, *The Lost Apocrypha of the Old Testament,* p. 9.

15. In an interpolation in the *Liber Floridus* of Lambertus, Canon of St. Omer, made, according to Meyer, after 1120 (Meyer, "Die Geschichte," pp. 119–20), we have the following narrative: Adam, about to die, told Seth he longed for the fragrance of the tree of knowledge. Seth went, as he was bidden, to the East and called upon God. From there he was carried to Paradise by an angel and returned with a branch of the tree of knowledge, which he gave Adam to smell. After Adam's death Seth planted the twig. (As in other versions, the tree was later used to make the cross.) This version has preserved details of what was probably a very old form of the Seth legend. The desire, for instance, of Adam to smell the tree is related to the ancient belief that life can be communicated by smelling a branch of the tree of life. Widengren ("The King and the Tree of Life," pp. 27, 30) referred to instances in Mesopotamian art in which a figure—probably intended to represent the divine king—raises to his nose a plant with three leaves (see von Oppenheim, *Der Tell Halaf,* p. 157, Pl. XXXVII). More explicit is a passage in one of the Sargonid letters, cited by Widengren, p. 21, in which the writer stated that "the King gave us life by means of placing the Plant of Life under our nose." According to Widengren, "the fact that this pattern occurs in Palestine . . . is important in tracing among the Israelites the idea of the Plant of Life or the twig from the Tree of Life" (Widengren, p. 30; see also Patai, p. 38).

16. Ginzberg, II, 291–93; V, 96. Rappoport, *The Folklore of the Jews,* p. 127; Rappoport, *Myth and Legend,* II, 254–57. Moses Gaster, *The Chronicles of Jerahmeel,* p. 121. See especially the version preserved in the Syriac *Book of the Bee,* ed. and trans. Budge, pp. 24, 50. See also Friedlander, *Pirkê de Rabbi Eliezer,* pp. 312–13.

17. Ginzberg, *Legends of the Jews,* III, 477.

18. Scholem, *Major Trends in Jewish Mysticism,* pp. 283, 415, n. 124. According to Scholem, it was partly printed in Mohilev in 1812 and is preserved in a more complete version in MS Oxford 1820. The section which concerns us was translated into Latin by Fabricius, *Codex pseudepigraphus veteris testamenti,* I, 80–81.

19. The taking of the branch by Jonitus represents the same notion translated to the time of the Flood: after all things had been destroyed by water, man again needed a vestige of the primeval paradise from which he had come.

20. Ginzberg, *Legends of the Jews*, V, 148–49 n. 50.

21. Issaverdens (trans.), *The Uncanonical Writings of the Old Testament*, pp. 72–73; Preuschen, "Die apokryphen gnostischen Adamschriften," p. 203.

22. Jung, *Symbols of Transformation*, p. 170. Cf. *Adam and Eve's eating the forbidden fruit.*

23. Simpson, "Genesis," *The Interpreter's Bible*, I, 494.

24. Cf. *1 Enoch* 25, in Charles, II, 204–5; *Testament of Levi* 18:10–11, in Charles, II, 315.

25. James, *The Apocryphal New Testament*, p. 127.

26. Charles, II, 124.

27. Jagić, "Slavische Beiträge zu den biblischen Apocryphen," pp. 6–8, 24–25, 55–56, 86–88; extant in two forms: in one version there are three twigs; in the other, one twig.

28. Moses Gaster, *Ilchester Lectures*, pp. 31–34.

29. *Ibid.*, p. 37. Cf. Wesselofsky, pp. 134–35.

30. Jagić, p. 56.

31. Moses Gaster, *Ilchester Lectures*, p. 155.

32. Charles, II, 125, 127.

33. Issaverdens, p. 78; Preuschen, p. 206.

34. Issaverdens, pp. 81–82; Preuschen, pp. 208–9.

35. Jacoby, "Kreuzbaum, Kreuzholz," col. 492.

36. Moses Gaster, *Ilchester Lectures*, p. 36.

37. Widengren, "The King and the Tree of Life," pp. 11–14, 19, 33–35, 47.

38. Frazer, I, 248, 309.

39. Farbridge, *Studies in Biblical and Semitic Symbolism*, pp. 206–7.

40. Virgil *Aeneid* vi.

41. Meyer, "Die Geschichte," pp. 115–16.

42. *Ibid.*, pp. 120–22.

43. Tertullian, *Carmina adversus Marcionem*, PL, Vol. II, col. 1067; Epiphanius, *Adversus haereses*, Bk. XLVI, chap. 5. Jerome, *Letters and Select Works*, p. 61.

44. Moses Gaster, *Ilchester Lectures*, p. 37.

45. Saewulf, *The Pilgrimage of Saewulf to Jerusalem*, pp. 11–12.

CHAPTER 6

1. Meyer, "Die Geschichte," pp. 128, 130.

2. Four Latin MSS were known to Meyer; Suchier, in his edition of the text, which he entitled "Post peccatum Ade," *Denkmäler provenzalischer Literatur und Sprache*, I, 165–200, listed seven additional MSS; Horstmann printed another MS in *Archiv für das Studium der neueren Sprachen*, LXXIX (1887), 459 ff. Napier listed all these MSS and added two more (*History of the Holy Rood-Tree*,

p. xxxi). For versions derived from the *Legende*, see Meyer, "Die Geschichte," pp. 149–65 and Napier, pp. xxxiii–xxxiv.

3. We have not considered the version in Jacobus de Voragine because it is important not for innovations but for continuing existent traditions. For instance, the part of the *Legenda Aurea* which appears in the *Legende* probably comes from Johannes Beleth. We shall have more to say of this point presently.

4. Meyer, "Die Geschichte," pp. 131–48.

5. Patch, *The Other World According to Descriptions in Medieval Literature*, p. 148.

6. *Ibid.*, p. 143.

7. *Ibid.*, p. 64.

8. Duine, "L'espace dénudé," p. 382; Vaugeois, "Contes et légendes de Fougères," p. 251; *The Denham Tracts*, ed. Hardy, II, 23; Patai, *Man and Temple*, p. 152; T. H. Gaster, *Thespis*, p. 296; see also Stith Thompson, III, 253. The reverse of this motif is also found, that blood (usually of a holy person) causes the grass to grow more greenly; *The Acts of Philip*, pp. 314–15; Bede, *The Ecclesiastical History of the English Nation*, Bk. III, chap. 10. Indeed this belief in the fertilizing effect of blood on vegetation may represent the older form of the motif; see also Stith Thompson, II, 488.

9. Courtney, "Cornish Folk-Lore," p. 43; Stith Thompson, II, 489; see also Hawthorne, *The Scarlet Letter*, chap. 11.

10. Jung, *Symbols of Transformation*, p. 315; Stith Thompson, II, 165; Frazer, *The Golden Bough*, I, 207–11; XIII, 63–66.

11. *The Mabinogion*, p. 301. The motif also appears in Hawthorne's *Scarlet Letter;* Hester looked to see whether "the tender grass of early spring would not be blighted" beneath the footsteps of Roger Chillingworth (chap. 15).

12. Heidel, *The Gilgamesh Epic and Old Testament Parallels*, pp. 8–10, 64–92.

13. Patch, pp. 64, 148.

14. Biblical commentators relate the cherubim of Gen. 2 to fabulous winged animals of Assyrian and Babylonian mythology (Ryle, "Cherubim"). See also Goblet d'Alviella, pp. 152–53.

15. Burkitt, *Jewish and Christian Apocalypses*, pp. 40–41.

16. Stith Thompson, V, 477; Patch, pp. 153–54.

17. Peebles, "The Dry Tree: Symbol of Death," pp. 59–79, and Bennett, "The Legend of the Green Tree and the Dry," pp. 21–32.

18. Yule (trans. and ed.), *The Book of Ser Marco Polo*, I, 134. The dry tree and the green also appear in Ezech. 20:47.

19. Bennett, p. 24.

20. King James version. According to Gilmour, *The Interpreter's Bible*, VIII, 405, the passage is a proverbial saying with many rabbinical parallels.

21. *The Apocalypse of Moses* 20:4, in Charles, II, 146. Ginzberg, *Legends of the Jews*, I, 96. Patai cites a Jewish legend in which the

fertility of the trees vanished when Cain killed Abel (p. 152); also Ginzberg, I, 112.

22. Ronald Knox (trans.).

23. Malan (ed. and trans.), *The Book of Adam and Eve*, p. 4.

24. Budge (ed. and trans.), "The Mysteries of St. John the Apostle and Holy Virgin," pp. 249–50; Peebles, "The Dry Tree," p. 73.

25. See chap. 5, n. 14.

26. Budge (ed. and trans.), *The History of Alexander the Great*, p. 101.

27. Peebles, "The Dry Tree," pp. 68–70.

28. Pfister (ed. and trans.), *Der Alexanderroman des Archipresbyters Leo*. English trans., Schlauch, *Medieval Narrative*, p. 317. See also Yule, I, 114. Miss Peebles, p. 71, refers to a similar vision of Bors; Malory, *Works*, Bk. XVI, chap. 6, p. 687, in which he sees a dry tree with a pelican in its branches. Cf. also in the "Squire's Tale" the tree which Canace sees, "for drye as whit as chalk" and in its branches a falcon (1. 409).

29. Peebles, "The Dry Tree," p. 59; see also pp. 60 ff.

30. *Ibid.*, p. 60.

31. *Ibid.*, p. 67; Yule, I, 127–28.

32. Peebles, p. 63; Cordier (ed.), *Les voyages en Asie au XIVe siècle du bienheureux frère Odoric de Pordenone*, p. 19.

33. Mandeville, *Travels*, I, 44. See Peebles, "The Dry Tree," pp. 64–66, for sources of this tradition.

34. Zarncke, "Der Priester Johannes," VII, 1010; VIII, 127–28; Jones, "The Squire's Tale," p. 359.

35. Greenhill, "The Child in the Tree," p. 356; Jacoby, "Kreuzbaum, Kreuzholz," col. 491.

36. Meyer, "Die Geschichte," p. 114, and cf. p. 107.

37. Among the most elaborate symbolic uses of the dry tree subsequent to the *Legende* is in Guillaume Deguilleville's *Le pèlerinage de l'âme*, pp. 185 ff. See Bennett, pp. 21 ff.

38. Frazer, *Folk-Lore in the Old Testament*, I, 45–77.

39. There is also a Judeo-Christian tradition of the serpent as the symbol of healing (see Num. 21:6–9 and John 3:14–15).

40. Watts, *Myth and Ritual in Christianity*, p. 79; Kramer, p. 19; van Buren, *Symbols of the Gods*, p. 40; Goblet d'Alviella, p. 133.

41. Frazer, *Folk-Lore in the Old Testament*, I, 45–77; Frazer, *The Belief in Immortality*, I, 69 ff., 74–75.

42. Goldsmith, *Life Symbols as Related to Sex Symbolism*, p. 113.

43. See, for instance, the vase reproduced by Goblet d'Alviella, p. 167, Fig. 83; see also Decharme, *Mythologie de la grèce antique*, p. 535, Fig. 140.

44. Goblet d'Alviella, Pl. IV, Fig. d, p. 123; Langdon (ed.), *The Mythology of All Races*, V (Semitic), Fig. 68, pp. 177, 179.

45. Twining, *Symbols and Emblems of Early and Mediaeval Christian Art*, p. 151, Pl. LXXV, Fig. 1.

46. Lowrie, *Monuments of the Early Church*, pp. 204, 256, 259, Fig. 95. Lowrie, *Art in the Early Church*, Plates 19*c*, 28, 115*b*, 150*b*, and 151*f*. Goblet d'Alviella, Pl. V, Fig. m.

47. The serpent of Seth's vision clearly symbolizes the Temptation and Fall of Man as it is related in Genesis. Whatever may have been the point of earlier texts of Genesis, in the text which has come down to us the cause of Man's Fall is his disobedience. See the interesting article by Gordis, "The Significance of the Paradise Myth," pp. 88–94, in which man's first sin is interpreted as sexual transgression.

48. Potvin (ed.), *Perceval le gallois ou le conte du graal*, V, ll. 33764 ff.

49. Roach (ed.), *The Didot Perceval According to the MSS of Modena and Paris*, p. 203 ff.; see also pp. 73–76, 125–30.

50. Stengel (ed.), *Li romans de Durmart de galois*, ll. 1537 ff., 15541 ff.

51. Weston, "The Apple Mystery in Arthurian Romance," pp. 417–30, esp. 425.

52. See Brugger, *The Illuminated Tree in Two Arthurian Romances*, pp. 77–93; Greenhill, "A Legend of Terrestrial Paradise in Wauchier's Continuation of the Conte du Graal," pp. 2–4; Eleanor Hull, review in *Folk-Lore*, XLI (1930), 400 ff.

53. Peebles, "The Children in the Tree," p. 294.

54. *Ibid.*, pp. 294, 297.

55. Brugger, p. 22; cf. also p. 32, pp. 84–85.

56. *Ibid.*, pp. 23–25.

57. Greenhill, "A Legend of Terrestrial Paradise," p. 14; cf. pp. 132, 133.

58. *Ibid.*, pp. 106–27, esp. 121–22.

59. *Ibid.*, p. 134 n. 2.

60. Cf. the change of *pedes asininos* in Eastern legends to *pedes anserinos* in the West (see chap. 4).

61. Brugger, p. 32; Greenhill, "A Legend of Terrestrial Paradise," p. 133.

62. Brugger, pp. 32, 325–26, 371.

63. Meyer, "Die Geschichte," p. 130.

64. Greenhill, "The Child in the Tree," p. 329.

65. *Ibid.*, p. 371.

66. There is evidence which suggests the possibility that there were versions of the Seth and rood-tree legend (including the vision of Paradise) which antedated the *Legende*. See, for instance, the Old French version in Graf, *Miti*, I, Appendix II, 218–28, which Graf dated, probably 12th century. According to Peebles, "The Dry Tree," p. 74 n. 44, "the earliest version [which includes the seared footsteps and Seth's three glimpses of Paradise] seems to be that in the *Image du monde* version, II, 1247"; Fant, *L'image du monde*, pp. 5–6, 31–32. There is also a very real possibility that the Latin *Legende* itself may be earlier than Meyer believed. Meyer's dating

the *Legende* after 1254 was based on his assumption that the author had used the *Legenda Aurea* as a source. Meyer gave as his reason for supposing the *Legende* to have derived material from the *Legenda Aurea*, the author's attempt to reconcile the contradictory accounts in Jacobus. These accounts are present in other and earlier versions which, moreover, correspond more closely to the *Legende* than do those of Jacobus. The problem needs a fuller investigation than is possible here. We shall take up the matter again when considering the motifs in the *Legende* which Meyer believed to have come from the *Legenda Aurea*. Baring-Gould, *Curious Myths of the Middle Ages*, summarizes a version which includes the scorched footprints and the three visions of Paradise, but lacks the Maximilla episode (pp. 379–83). Since he does not indicate his source, it is not clear whether this version is a synthetic one or a real one; if it is an authentic version, it might represent an earlier form of the *Legende*.

67. Watson, *The Early Iconography of the Tree of Jesse*, pp. 1–7; see esp. Plates V and XV, also VI, VII, and X and pp. 89–90, 99–102.

68. Greenhill, "The Child in the Tree," p. 329 n. 20; Bergema, *De Boom des Levens in Schrift en Historie*, p. 510; Patch, p. 156; Jacoby, cols. 491–92.

69. Greenhill, p. 336; Herrman, *Ezeckiel übersetzt und erklärt*, p. 107; Heinisch, *Das Buch Ezechiel übersetzt und erklärt*, p. 90; Jacoby, p. 490.

70. In at least one instance, a whole small nativity scene has been included in the tree: window, 2d half of 13th century at Darmstadt (see The Christian Art Index at Princeton University).

71. Watson, Plates IX, XII, XV ff.; Ferguson, pp. 50–51.

72. Müller (ed.), *The Mythology of All Races*, XII (Egyptian), 35, Fig. 21.

73. *Ibid.*, p. 39.

74. Viau, "Egyptian Mythology," pp. 23–24.

75. Müller, pp. 92–93, Fig. 84.

76. *Ibid.*, pp. 165–66; Fig. 176 shows the bird resting in the tree.

77. Dussaud, "Notes de mythologie syrienne," p. 378; Barlow, "Sacred Trees," p. 274; Viau, p. 13.

78. Van Buren, *Symbols of the Gods*, pp. 24–25. Cf. the Egyptian representation of the sun disc at the top of the sacred tree (Müller, p. 35, Fig. 21).

79. Sayce, *The Religion of the Ancient Babylonians*, pp. 238–39; Goblet d'Alviella, pp. 156–57.

80. Goblet d'Alviella, p. 204; Langdon, *The Mythology of All Races*, V, 58–60; Lajard, "Recherches sur le culte du cyprès pyramidal chez les peuples civilisés de l'antiquité," Pl. I, Fig. 2; Dussaud, p. 377.

81. Dussaud, p. 377.

82. It is well known that pagan art provided models for Christian art. As early as the second century the figure of the good shepherd

appeared in the catacombs, modeled on the pagan statues of Hermes Criophoros. Lowrie, *Art in the Early Church,* p. 92. Cf. pp. 61–62, 69; Goblet d'Alviella, p. 94.

83. See in Dussaud a bronze representation of the young sun-god emerging from the branches (pp. 378–79). Delaporte, "Phoenician Mythology," p. 81.

84. Goblet d'Alviella, p. 142.

85. On a liturgical comb, attributed to St. Lupus, dated between 7th and 13th centuries, in the treasury of St. Etienne at Sens (Maskell, *Ivories,* p. 209).

86. See, for instance, the 6th-century mosaic in Santa Prassede (Bennett, p. 32); a mosaic in the Church of Santa Cecilia at Rome, 820 (Twining, p. 180, Pl. LXXXIX, Fig. 7; Morey, *Early Christian Art,* p. 171).

87. On a tympanum at Croxdale Church (Keyser, *A List of Norman Tympana and Lintels,* Fig. 93, p. xxxviii).

88. Aubert, *La Bourgogne. La sculpture,* II, Pl. 108, p. 41.

89. Twining, p. 154, Pl. LXXVI, Fig. 11.

90. Widengren, "The King and the Tree of Life," p. 57 n. 3.

91. For an interesting survival, not only of the concept of the cosmological tree but, of the idea that the deity rested in the tree, see the 4th-century *Apocalyse of Paul,* in James, *The Apocryphal New Testament,* p. 549.

92. Greenhill, "The Child in the Tree," pp. 329, 331.

93. *Ibid.,* p. 371.

94. Piper, "The Tree of Life," *Journal of Sacred Literature,* VI, 37–38, 47–50; Bergema, pp. 503–12; Bauerreis, *Arbor Vitae: Der Lebensbaum und seine Verwendung in Liturgie, Kunst, und Brauchtum des Abendlandes,* pp. 7–11.

95. Piper, "The Tree of Life," *Journal of Sacred Literature,* IV, 393; VI, 27–28; VIII, 59–60.

96. Raby, *A History of Christian Latin Poetry,* p. 365.

97. *Ibid.,* p. 366. One of the most popular images for Mary among the hymn-writers—as among the liturgical artists—was the tree of Jesse, an association which was undoubtedly fostered by the similarity between *virgo* (virgin) and *virga* (rod).

98. Piper, "The Tree of Life," *Journal of Sacred Literature,* VI, 29–30; Dreves (ed.), *Analecta hymnica medii aevi,* XXXV, 137.

99. Dreves, XXXV, 172.

100. Of interest, too, are the frequent representations in early Christian art of Christ on the top of the world (Morey, pp. 135, 142, 145, 166, 169, 172, Fig. 177). Here we are not far from the sun god on the top of the world tree.

101. Goblet d'Alviella, p. 12.

102. George Birdwood, pp. viii–ix, in Goblet d'Alviella's *The Migration of Symbols.* Goblet d'Alviella illustrated his thesis by tracing the migration of a number of symbols, for instance, the swastika, the caduceus, and the sacred tree; see esp. pp. 118–76 on the sym-

bolism and mythology of the tree. See also Goodenough, *Jewish Symbols in the Greco-Roman Period*, VII, 87–134.

103. Jung, p. xxix.

104. *Ibid.*, p. 158; see esp. pp. 219, 242, 246–47.

105. Meyer, in citing Geoffrey as the source, is certainly mistaken since there is no mention of seeds in Geoffrey, and the twigs are cypress, fir, and palm, not cypress, cedar, and pine, as in the *Legende* and in the Bodleian version.

106. Kohler, "Apple," *Jewish Encyclopedia*, II, 23–24.

107. Delitzsch, *Biblischer Commentar über das Alte Testament,* IV, Pt. 4, 127.

108. Piper, *Mythologie und Symbolik der christlichen Kunst*, I, 67–75; see also Graves, *The Greek Myths*, II, 145–46, and Goblet d'Alviella, pp. 131–32. For the apple in Celtic and Teutonic myth, see Patch, p. 31, and MacCulloch, *Mythology of All Races*, II (Eddic), 22.

109. It does not appear in all texts. See, for instance, Mozley, p. 141.

110. Meyer, "Die Geschichte," p. 128.

111. *Ibid.*, p. 129.

112. *Ibid.*

113. Dunbar, *A Dictionary of Saintly Women*, II, 82; *Acta sanctorum*, Feb. III, 132.

114. James, *The Apocryphal New Testament*, pp. 348–49.

115. Hippolytus, *The Refutation of All Heresies*, Bk. VIII, chap. xii, 123; Tertullian, *Against Praxeas*, chap. i, 597; Eusebius, *Church History*, Bk. V, chaps. xiv–xvi, 229–33.

116. As Napier pointed out (pp. xiv, xxxv, xli, xliii, xliv–xlvi), and as we observed in chap. 3, the *Legende* and the Bodleian MS both go back to a common source.

117. Actually a pool; see 2 *Esdras* 3:15; John 9:7, 11.

118. Meyer, "Die Geschichte," pp. 115–16; cf. chap. 4.

119. Meyer, Die Geschichte," p. 148; chap. 4.

BIBLIOGRAPHY

AARNE, ANTTI. *Verzeichnis der Märchentypen.* "Folklore Fellows Communications," No. 3. Helsinki, 1910. Trans. and enlarged by STITH THOMPSON, *The Types of the Folk-Tale.* "Folklore Fellows Communications," No. 74. Helsinki, 1928.

Acta sanctorum. Ed. JOANNES BOLLANDUS and GODEFRIDUS HENSCHENIUS. Paris, 1865. February III.

AELIANUS. *Varia historia.* Ed. RUDOLPH HERCHER. Paris, 1858.

ALBRIGHT, WILLIAM FOXWELL. "The Location of the Garden of Eden," *American Journal of Semitic Languages and Literatures,* XXXIX (1922–23), 15–30.

———. "The Mouth of the Rivers," *ibid.,* XXXV (1918–19), 161–95.

———. *From the Stone Age to Christianity.* 2d ed. Baltimore, 1957.

ALEXANDER MONACHUS. *De inventione sanctae crucis. PG,* Vol. LXXXVII.

AMBROSE. *Expositionis in Lucam. PL,* Vol. XV.

——. *Letters.* Trans. SISTER MARY MELCHIOR BEYENKA. "The Fathers of the Church," Vol. XXVI. New York, 1954.

AMES, RUTH MARGARET. "The Debate between the Church and the Synagogue." Ph.D. dissertation, Columbia University, 1950.

ANASTASIUS SINAITICA. *Anagogicarum contemplationum in hexaemeron. PG,* Vol. LXXXIX.

——. *De trinitate.* "Thesaurus monumentorum ecclesiasticorum et historicorum," I, 436–47. Amsterdam, 1725.

ANDREAS CRETENSIS. *In exaltationem sanctae crucis. I. PG,* Vol. XCVII.

ANWANDER, ANTON. "Das Kreuz Christi und andere Kreuze," *Theologische Quartalsschrift,* CXV (1934), 491–515.

ASHTON, JOHN. *The Legendary History of the Cross.* New York, 1887.

ATHANASIUS (DUBIA). *De passione et cruce domini. PG,* Vol. XXVIII.

ATKINSON, ROBERT (ed.). *The Passions and the Homilies from Leabhar Breac.* "Todd Lecture Series," Vol. II. Dublin, 1887.

AUBERT, MARCEL. *La Bourgogne. La sculpture.* Vol. II. Paris, 1930.

AUGUSTINE. *The City of God.* Trans. MARCUS DODS. New York, 1950.

——. *Sermo I, Sermo LXXXIV. PL,* Vol. XXXIX.

BACHMANN, FRIEDRICH. *Die beiden Versionen des me. Canticum de creatione.* Hamburg, 1891.

BARING-GOULD, S. *Curious Myths of the Middle Ages.* Philadelphia, 1869.

BARLOW, H. C. "Sacred Trees," *Journal of Sacred Literature,* I (1862), 273–92.

Barnabas, Epistle of. "Ante-Nicene Christian Library," Vol. I. Edinburgh, 1867.

BARTHÉLEMY, O. P., and MILIK, J. T. *Qumran Cave I.* Oxford, 1955.

BASIL. *Enarratio in prophetam Isaiam. PG,* Vol. XXX.

BAUERREIS, ROMUALD. *Arbor Vitae: Der Lebensbaum und seine Verwendung in Liturgie, Kunst, und Brachtum des Abendlands.* Munich, 1938.

BEICHNER, PAUL E. "The *Cursor mundi* and Petrus Riga," *Speculum,* XXIV (1949), 239–50.

——. "The Old French Verse *Bible* of Macé de la Charité, a Translation of the *Aurora*," *ibid.*, XXII (1947), 226–39.

BENNETT, M. R. "The Legend of the Green Tree and the Dry," *Archaeological Journal*, LXXXIII (1926), 21–32.

BERGEMA, HENDRIK. *De Boom des Levens in Schrift en Historie.* Hilversum, 1938.

BERGER, SAMUEL. *La bible français au moyen âge.* Paris, 1884.

BERJEAU, JEAN PHILIBERT. *Geschiedenis van het heylighe Cruyz.* London, 1863.

BERLINGER, ANTON. "Legenden," *Theologisches Literaturblatt* (Bonn), Vol. VI (1871).

BERNARD, J. H. "The Descent into Hades and Christian Baptism," *Studia sacra* (London), 1917, pp. 1–50.

—— (ed.). *The Odes of Solomon.* "Texts and Studies," Vol. VIII, No. 3. Cambridge, 1912.

BEZOLD, CARL. "Das arabisch-äthiopische Testamentum Adami, *Orientalische Studien*, II (1906).

—— (ed. and trans.). "Kebra Nagast. Die Herrlichkeit der Könige," *Abhandlungen der philosophisch-philologischen Klasse der Königlich Bayerischen Akademie der Wissenschaften* (Munich), Vol. XXIII, Pt. 1. (1909).

—— (ed. and trans.). *Die Schatzhöle.* Leipzig, 1883.

BLISS, A. J. "The Auchinleck *Life of Adam and Eve*," *Review of English Studies*, VII (1956), 406–9.

BLOCH, JOSHUA. "On the Apocalyptic in Judaism," *Jewish Quarterly Review*, N.S. II (1952), 1–153.

——. "Outside Books," in *Mordecai M. Kaplan Jubilee Volume*, ed. MOSHE DAVIS, I, 87–108. New York, 1953.

BOCHART, SAMUEL. *Geographia sacra seu Phaleg et Canaan. Opera omnia.* Vol. I. 4th ed. Lyons, 1712.

BOLTE, JOHANNES, and POLÍVKA, GEORG. *Anmerkungen zu den Kinder- und Hausmärchen der Brüder Grimm.* Vol. II. Leipzig, 1915.

BONNARD, JEAN. *Les traductions de la bible en vers français au moyen âge.* Paris, 1884.

BORLAND, LOIS. "Herman's *Bible*, and the *Cursor mundi*," *Studies in Philology*, XXX (1933), 427–44.

BOUSSET, WILHELM. "Platons Weltseele und das Kreuz Christi," *Zeitschrift für die neutestamentliche Wissenschaft*, XIV (1913), 273–85.

——. *Die Religion des Judentums.* 3d ed. Rev. H. GRESSMANN. Tübingen, 1926.

Bibliography 167

BOVENSCHEN, ALBERT. *Die Quellen für die Reisenbeschreibung des Johann von Mandeville.* Berlin, 1888.

BOX, G. H. (ed.). *Apocalypse of Abraham.* New York, 1918.

BRÉHIER, LOUIS. *L'art chrétien.* 2d ed. Paris, 1928.

BRUGGER, E. *The Illuminated Tree in Two Arthurian Romances.* New York: Institute of French Studies, 1929.

BUDGE, ERNEST A. WALLIS. *The History of Alexander the Great.* Cambridge, 1889.

———. "The Mysteries of St. John the Apostle and Holy Virgin," in *Coptic Apocrypha in the Dialect of Upper Egypt.* London, 1913.

———. *The Queen of Sheba and Her Only Son Menyelek.* 2d ed. London, 1932.

——— (ed. and trans.). *The Book of the Bee.* "Anecdota Oxoniensia, Semitic Series," Vol. I, Pt. 2. Oxford, 1886.

BUREN, E. DOUGLAS VAN. *The Flowing Vase and the God with Streams.* Berlin, 1933.

———. *Symbols of the Gods in Mesopotamian Art.* Rome, 1945.

BURKITT, F. CRAWFORD. *Church and Gnosis.* Cambridge, 1932.

———. *Jewish and Christian Apocalypses.* London, 1914.

———. *The Religion of the Manichees.* Cambridge, 1925.

BURSTEIN, SONA ROSA. "The Harrowing of Hell," *Folk-Lore,* XXXIX (1928), 113–32.

BUTLER, PIERCE. *Legenda aurea—Légende dorée—Golden Legend.* Baltimore, 1899.

BUTTENWEISER, MOSES. "Books of Adam," in *The Universal Jewish Encyclopedia,* I, 78–79. New York, 1939.

CASSEL, PAULUS. *Das Buch Esther.* Berlin, 1878. Trans. AARON BERNSTEIN, *Explanatory Commentary on Esther.* Edinburgh, 1888.

CASSIODORUS. *Historia tripartita. PL,* Vol. LXIX.

CAXTON, WILLIAM. *The Golden Legend or Lives of the Saints as Englished by William Caxton.* Ed. F. S. ELLIS. Vols. I and III. London, 1931–34.

CERIANI, ANTONIUS (ed.). "Apocalypsis Moysi," *Monumenta sacra et profana,* V (1868), 19–24.

CHAMBERS, E. K. *Arthur of Britain.* London, 1927.

CHARLES, R. H. (ed.). *The Apocrypha and Pseudephigrapha of the Old Testament.* Vol. II (Pseudepigrapha). Oxford, 1913.

CHASE, FREDERIC HENRY. *Confirmation in the Apostolic Age.* London, 1913.

CHRYSOSTOM. *De adoratione pretiosae crucis.* (Spuria). *PG,* Vol. LII.

———. *Commentarius in sanctum Joannem. Homilia LXXXV.* PG, Vol. LIX.

COMBES, LOUIS DE. *The Finding of the Cross.* Trans. LUIGI CAP- PADELTA. "International Catholic Library," ed. Rev. J. WIL- HELM, Vol. X. New York, 1907.

COMPARETTI, DOMENICO. *Vergil in the Middle Ages.* Trans. E. F. M. BENECKE. London, 1895.

CONYBEARE, FRED C. "On the Apocalypse of Moses," *Jewish Quarterly Review*, VII (1894-95), 216-35.

COOKE, ALBERT S. (ed.). *The Old English Elene, Phoenix, and Physiologus.* New Haven, 1919.

CORBLET, L'ABBÉ J. "Étude iconographique sur l'arbre de Jesse," *Revue de l'art chrétien*, IV (1860), 49-61, 113-25, 169-81.

CORDIER, HENRI (ed.). *Les voyages en Asie au XIVe siècle du bienheureux frère Odoric de Pardenone.* Paris, 1891.

COURTNEY, M. A. "Cornish Folk-Lore," *Folk-Lore Journal*, V (1887).

CRAIG, HARDIN. *English Religious Drama of the Middle Ages.* Oxford, 1955.

CRAWLEY, A. E. "Anointing," *Encyclopaedia of Religion and Ethics*, I, 549-54. New York, 1913.

CROSS, F. L. (ed.). *St. Cyril of Jerusalem's Lectures on the Sac- raments.* London, 1951.

CROSS, SAMUEL H. "The Earliest Allusion in Slavic Literature to the *Revelations* of Pseudo-Methodius," *Speculum*, IV (1929), 329-39.

CROTTY, GENEVIEVE. "The Exeter 'Harrowing of Hell': A Re- Interpretation," *PMLA*, LIV (1939), 349-58.

CUMONT, FRANZ. *After Life in Roman Paganism.* New Haven, 1922.

———. "La cosmogonie manichéenne d'après Théodore bar Khôni," *Recherches sur le manichéisme.* Brussels, 1908.

CURTIUS, ERNST ROBERT. *Europäische Literatur und lateinisches Mittelalter.* Bern, 1948. Trans. WILLARD TRASK, *European Literature and the Latin Middle Ages.* New York, 1953.

CYPRIAN. "De Pascha," *S. Thasci Caecili Cypriani opera omnia.* Ed. W. HARTEL. "Corpus scriptorum ecclesiasticorum Lati- norum," III, Pt. 3, 305-8. Vienna, 1871.

DAICHES, SAMUEL. *Babylonian Oil Magic in the Talmud and in the Later Jewish Literature.* London, 1913.

DANTHINE, HÉLÈNE. *Le palmier—dattier et les arbres sacrés.* Paris, 1937.

DARNEDDE, LOTHAR. *Deutsche Sibyllen-Weissagung.* Charlot- tenburg, 1933.

DAY, MABEL (ed.). "Life of Adam and Eve," *The Wheatly Manuscript.* EETS, CLV, 76–99. London, 1921.

DECHARME, P. *Mythologie de la grèce antique.* 2d ed. Paris, 1886.

DELAPORTE, L. "Phoenician Mythology," *Larousse Encyclopedia of Mythology,* pp. 73–86. New York, 1959.

DELITZSCH, FRANZ. *Biblischer Commentar über das Alte Testament.* Vol. IV, Pt. 4. Leipzig, 1875. Trans. M. G. EASTON, *Commentary on the Song of Songs and Ecclesiastes.* Edinburgh, 1877.

D'EVELYN, CHARLOTTE, and MILL, ANNA J. (eds.). *The South English Legendary.* EETS, Vols. CCXXXV, CCXXXVI, CCXLIV. London, 1956.

DIDRON, ADOLPHE NAPOLÉON. *Christian Iconography.* Trans. E. J. MILLINGTON. Vol. I. London, 1886.

———. *Manuel d'iconographie chrétienne grecque et latine.* Paris, 1845.

DILLMAN, A. *Das christliche Adambuch des Morgenlandes.* Göttingen, 1853.

DOBSCHÜTZ, ERNST VON. "Nicodemus, Gospel of," *A Dictionary of the Bible,* III, 544–47. New York, 1901.

DREVES, GUIDO MARIA (ed.). *Analecta hymnica medii aevi.* Vol. XXXV. Leipzig, 1900.

DUFF, GORDON (ed.). *The Dialogue or Communing between the Wise King Solomon and Marcolphus.* London, 1892.

DUINE, F. "L'espace dénudé," *Revue des traditions populaires,* XVIII (1903).

DU MÉRIL, EDELSTAND. *Les origines latines du théatre moderne.* Paris, 1897.

DUNBAR, AGNES B. C. *A Dictionary of Saintly Women.* Vol. II. London, 1905.

DUNSTAN, A. C. "The Middle English Canticum de Creatione and the Latin *Vita Adae et Evae,*" *Anglia,* LV (1931), 431–42.

DUSSAUD, RENÉ. "Notes de mythologie syrienne," *Revue archéologique,* 4th ser., I (1903), 347–82.

EISSFELDT, OTTO. *Einleitung in das Alte Testament.* 2d ed. Tübingen, 1956.

ELIADE, MIRCEA. *Patterns in Comparative Religion.* Trans. ROSEMARY SHEED. New York, 1958.

ENGNELL, IVAN. *Studies in Divine Kingship in the Ancient Near East.* Uppsala, 1943.

EPHRAIM SYRUS. *Homily on Our Lord.* "A Select Library of Nicene and Post-Nicene Fathers," 2d ser., Vol. XIII. New York, 1898.

EPIPHANIUS. *Adversus haereses. PG,* Vol. XLI.

EUSEBIUS. *Church History and The Oration in Praise of Constantine.* "A Select Library of Nicene and Post-Nicene Fathers," 2d ser., Vol. I. New York, 1890.

EWALD, HEINRICH. *Geschichte des Volkes Israel bis Christus.* Vol. III. 2d ed. Göttingen, 1853. Trans. J. ESTLIN CARPENTER, *The History of Israel.* London, 1871.

FABRICIUS, JOHANN ALBERT. *Codex apocryphus novi testamenti.* Vol. I. Hamburg, 1719.

————. *Codex pseudepigraphus veteris testamenti.* 2 vols. 2d ed. Hamburg, 1722.

FANT, CARL. *L'image du monde.* Uppsala, 1886.

FARBRIDGE, MAURICE H. *Studies in Biblical and Semitic Symbolism.* London, 1923.

FERGUSON, GEORGE. *Signs and Symbols in Christian Art.* 2d ed. New York, 1955.

FERRAR, WILLIAM JOHN. *The Uncanonical Jewish Books.* New York, 1918.

FÖRSTER, MAX. "Zum altenglischen Nicodemus-Evangelium," *Archiv für das Studium der neueren Sprachen,* CVII (1901), 311–21.

————. "Der Inhalt der altenglischen Handschrift Vesp. D. XIV," *Englische Studien,* LIV (1920), 46–68.

FOSTER, FRANCES A. (ed.). *The Northern Passion.* EETS, Vols. CXLV, CXLVII. London, 1913–16.

————. *A Stanzaic Life of Christ.* EETS, Vol. CLXVI. London, 1926.

FOX, NORMAN. "Baptism," *The New Schaff-Herzog Encyclopedia of Religious Knowledge,* I, 435–54. Grand Rapids, Mich., 1949.

FRANK, GRACE. *The Medieval French Drama.* Oxford, 1954.

FRAZER, JAMES GEORGE. *The Belief in Immortality.* Vol. I. London, 1913.

————. *Folk-Lore in the Old Testament.* Vol. I. London, 1919.

————. *The Golden Bough.* 13 vols. 3d ed. London, 1955.

FRIEDLANDER, GERALD. *Pirkê de Rabbi Eliezer.* London, 1916.

FROST, STANLEY BRICE. *Old Testament Apocalyptic.* London, 1952.

GASTER, MOSES. *The Chronicles of Jerahmeel.* London, 1899.

GASTER, MOSES. *Ilchester Lectures on Greeko*[sic]*-Slavonic Literature*. London, 1887.
——. *Literatura populară romăna*. Bucharest, 1883.
——. "Zur Quellenkunde deutscher Sagen und Märchen," *Germania*, XXV (1880), 274–94.
——. *Studies and Texts*. Vol. I. London, 1925–28.
GASTER, THEODOR H. "The Canaanite Epic of Keret," *Jewish Quarterly Review*, N.S., XXXVII (1946–47), 285–93.
——. *The Holy and the Profane*. New York, 1955.
——. "Myth and Story," *Numen*, I (1954), 184–212.
——. *The Oldest Stories in the World*. New York, 1952.
——. *Thespis*. New York, 1950.
—— (ed.). *The New Golden Bough*. New York, 1959.
GAYLEY, CHARLES MILLS. *Plays of Our Forefathers*. New York, 1907.
GEOFFREY OF VITERBO. *Pantheon*. "Rerum germanicarum scriptores," Vol. II: Johann Pistorius and Burcardo Gotthelff Struvius. Ratisbon, 1726.
GEORGIUS CEDRENUS. *Historiarum compendium*. *PG*, Vols. CXXI, CXXII.
GEORGIUS MONACHUS. *Chronicon*. *PG*, Vol. CX.
GEORGIUS SYNCELLUS. *Chronographia*. Ed. G. DINDORF. "Corpus scriptorum historiae byzantinae," Vol. XII. Bonn, 1829.
GEROULD, GORDON HALL. *Saints' Legends*. New York, 1916.
GERVASIUS VON TILBURY. *Otia imperalia*. Ed. FELIX LIEBRECHT. Hanover, 1856.
——. *Otia imperialia*. Ed. GOTTFRIED WILHELM LEIBNITZ. "Scriptores rerum brunsvicensium," Vol. I. Hanover, 1707.
GILMOUR, S. MACLEAN. "The Gospel According to St. Luke," in *The Interpreter's Bible*, VIII, 3–434. New York, 1952.
GINSBERG, HAROLD L. "The Legend of King Keret," *Bulletin of the American Schools of Oriental Research*, Supplementary Studies, Nos. 2–3. New Haven, 1946.
GINZBERG, LOUIS. "Book of Adam," *Jewish Encyclopedia*, I, 179–80. New York, 1901.
——. "Die Haggada bei den Kirchenvätern und in der apokryphischen Litteratur," *Monatsschrift für Geschichte und Wissenschaft des Judenthmus*. XLII (1898) and XLIII (1899).
——. *The Legends of the Jews*. 7 vols. Philadelphia, 1911–38.
——. *On Jewish Law and Lore*. Philadelphia, 1955.
GOBLET D'ALVIELLA, EUGÈNE. *La migration des symboles*. Paris, 1891. *The Migration of Symbols*. New York, 1956. (References are to the English translation.)

GOLDSMITH, ELIZABETH. *Life Symbols as Related to Sex Symbolism.* New York, 1924.

GOODENOUGH, ERWIN R. *Jewish Symbols in the Greco-Roman Period.* Vol. VII. "Bollingen Series," Vol. XXXVII. New York, 1958.

GOPPELT, LEONHARD. *Typos. Die typologische Deutung des Alten Testaments in Neuen.* Gütersloh, 1939.

GORDIS, ROBERT. "The Significance of the Paradise Myth," *American Journal of Semitic Languages and Literatures,* LII (1935–36), 86–94.

———. *The Song of Songs.* New York, 1954.

GORDON, CYRUS H. *Ugaritic Literature.* Rome, 1949.

GRADON, P. O. E. (ed.). *Cynewulf's Elene.* London, 1958.

GRAF, ARTURO. *La leggenda del paradiso terrestre.* Rome, 1878.

———. *Miti, leggende e superstizioni del medio evo.* Vol. I. Turin, 1892.

GRAVES, ROBERT. *The Greek Myths.* 2 vols. Baltimore, 1955.

GREENHILL, ELEANOR SIMMONS. "The Child in the Tree," *Traditio,* X (1954), 323–71.

———. "A Legend of Terrestrial Paradise in Wauchier's Continuation of the *Conte du Graal,*" M.A. thesis, Columbia University, 1945.

GREGORIUS NAZIANZENUS. *Carminum liber II historica. PG,* Vol. XXXVII.

GREGORY OF TOURS. *De gloria martyrum. PL,* Vol. LXXI.

GRETSER, JACOB. *De sancta cruce. Opera omnia.* Vol. II. Ratisbon, 1734.

GRIMM, JACOB. *Deutsche Mythologie.* 3 vols. 4th ed. Berlin, 1875–78. Trans. JAMES STEVEN STALLYBRASS, *Teutonic Mythology.* 4 vols. London, 1880–88.

Grimms' Fairy Tales. Trans. MARGARET HUNT, rev. JAMES STERN. New York, 1944.

GRÜNBAUM, M. *Neue Beiträge zur semitischen Sagenkunde.* Leiden, 1893.

GUBERNATIS, ANGELO DE. *La mythologie des plantes.* Vol. I. Paris, 1878.

GUÉNON, RENÉ. *Symbolism of the Cross.* Trans. ANGUS MACNAB. London, 1958.

GUILLAUME DE DEGUILEVILLE. *Le pèlerinage de l'âme.* Ed. J. J. STÜRZINGER. London, 1895.

GUIRAND, F. "Greek Mythology," in *Larousse Encyclopedia of Mythology,* pp. 87–212. New York, 1959.

HAIGHT, ELIZABETH HAZLETON (trans. and ed.). *The Life of*

Alexander of Macedon by Pseudo-Callisthenes. New York, 1955.

HALLIDAY, F. E. (trans.). *The Legend of the Rood.* London, 1955.

HAMMER-PURGSTALL. *Rosenöl.* Vol. I. Stuttgart and Tübingen, 1813.

HANAUER, J. E. *Folk-Lore of the Holy Land.* London, 1935.

HARDY, JAMES (ed.). *The Denham Tracts.* Vol. II. London, 1895.

HARNACK, ADOLF. *Geschichte der altchristlichen Literatur bis Eusebius.* 2 vols. 2d ed. Leipzig, 1958.

HAUPT, JOSEF. *Untersuchungen zur deutschen Saga.* Vol. I. Vienna, 1866.

HEIDEL, ALEXANDER. *The Gilgamesh Epic and Old Testament Parallels.* 2d ed. Chicago, 1949.

HEINISCH, PAUL. *Das Buch Ezechiel übersetzt und erklärt.* Bonn, 1923. Trans. WILLIAM G. HEIDT, *Christ in Prophecy.* St. Paul, Minn., 1956.

HERMANN, JOHANNES. *Ezeckiel übersetzt und erklärt.* Leipzig, 1924.

HERMAS. *The Pastor of Hermas.* "The Ante-Nicene Fathers," Vol. III. Grand Rapids, Mich., 1956.

HERODOTUS. Trans. A. D. GODLEY. Vol. I. Loeb ed. Cambridge, Mass., 1946.

HERR, JEANNE LUCIEN. "La reine de Saba et le bois de la croix," *Revue archéologique,* 4th ser., XXIII (1914), 1–31.

HERRADE DE LANDSBERG. *Hortus deliciarum.* Ed. A. STRAUB and G. KELLER. 2 vols. Strasbourg, 1901.

HERTZ, WILHELM. "Die Rätsel der Königin von Saba," *Zeitschrift für deutsches Alterthum und deutsche Literatur.* (Berlin) XXVII (1883), 1–33.

HEUSER, WILHELM, and FOSTER, FRANCES A. (eds.). *The Northern Passion.* EETS, Vol. CLXXXIII (Supplement). London, 1930.

HIPPOLYTUS. *The Refutation of All Heresies.* "The Ante-Nicene Fathers," Vol. V. Grand Rapids, Mich., 1951.

HIRSCH, EMIL G. "Esther. In Rabbinical Literature," *Jewish Encyclopedia,* V, 233–35. New York, 1903.

HIRSCH, FERDINAND. *Byzantinische Studien.* Leipzig, 1876.

HOLMBERG, UNO. "Der Baum des Lebens," *Suomalaisen Tiedeakatemian Toimituksia* (Helsinki), Ser. B, XVI (1922–23), 1–157.

—— (ed.). *Mythology of All Races,* Vol. IV (Siberian). Boston, 1927.

HOLMES, URBAN T., JR. (ed.). *Adenet le Rois' Berte aus grans piés.* "University of North Carolina Studies in the Romance Languages and Literature," No. 6. Chapel Hill, 1946.

HONORIUS OF AUTUN. *De imagine mundi. PL,* Vol. CLXXII.

————. *De inventione sanctae crucis. Speculum ecclesiae. PL,* Vol. CLXXII.

HOOKE, S. H. (ed.). *The Labyrinth.* London, 1935.

————. *Myth and Ritual.* London, 1933.

————. "Some Parallels with the Gilgamesh Story," *Folk-Lore,* XLV (1934), 195–211.

HORSTMANN, CARL (ed.). "Canticum de Creatione," *Anglia,* I (1878), 287–331.

————. "Canticum de Creatione," "Lyff of Adam and Eve," *Sammlung altenglischer Legenden.* Heilbronn, 1878.

————. *The Early South English Legendary.* EETS, Vol. LXXXVII. London, 1887.

————. "Vita prothoplausti Ade," "De ligno sce crucis," *Archiv für das Studium der neueren Sprachen,* LXXIX (1887), 459–69.

HOWARD, WILBERT F. "Exegesis of the Gospel According to St. John," in *The Interpreter's Bible,* Vol. VIII. New York, 1952.

HUCHER, EUGENE (ed.). *Le saint-graal.* Vol. I. Le Mans, 1875.

HULME, WILLIAM HENRY (ed.). *The Middle English Harrowing of Hell and Gospel of Nicodemus.* EETS, Vol. C. London, 1907.

————. "The Old English Gospel of Nicodemus," *Modern Philology,* I (1903–4), 579–614.

————. "The Old English Version of the Gospel of Nicodemus," *PMLA,* XIII (1898), 457–541.

IRENAEUS. *Against Heresies.* "The Ante-Nicene Fathers," Vol. I. Grand Rapids, Mich., 1956.

ISSAVERDENS, JACQUES (trans.). *The Uncanonical Writings of the Old Testament.* Venice. 1901.

JACOBUS DE VORAGINE. *Legenda aurea.* Ed. TH. GRAESSE. 3d ed. Bratislava, 1890.

————. *The Golden Legend.* Trans. GRANGER RYAN and HELMUT RIPPERGER. 2 vols. London, 1941.

JACOBY, ADOLF. "Kreuzbaum, Kreuzholz," *Handwörterbuch des deutschen Aberglaubens,* V (1933), 487–99.

JAGIĆ, VATROSLAV. "Slavische Beiträge zu den biblischen apocryphen," *Denkschriften der Kaiserlichen Akademie der Wissenschaften philosophisch-historische Classe* (Vienna), Vol. XLII (1893).

JAMES, E. O. *Myth and Ritual in the Ancient Near East.* London, 1958.

JAMES, MONTAGUE RHODES. *Apocrypha anecdota.* 2d ser., "Texts and Studies," Vol. V. Cambridge, 1897.

———. *The Lost Apocrypha of the Old Testament.* New York, 1920.

——— (trans.). *The Apocryphal New Testament.* Oxford, 1953.

JAMESON, ANNA. *History of Our Lord.* Vol. II. 2d ed. London, 1865.

JANSEN, H. LUDIN. *Die Henochgestalt: Eine vergleichende religionsgeschichte Untersuchung.* Oslo, 1939.

JASTROW, MORRIS, JR. "Anointing (Semitic)," *Encyclopaedia of Religion and Ethics,* I, 555–57. New York, 1913.

———. *The Civilization of Babylonia and Assyria.* Philadelphia, 1915.

———. *The Religion of Babylonia and Assyria.* Boston, 1898.

JEAN D'OUTREMEUSE. *Ly myreur des histors.* Ed. AD. BORGNET. Vol. I. Brussels, 1864.

JEREMIAS, ALFRED. *Das Alte Testament im Lichte des alten Orients.* 4th ed. Leipzig, 1930. 2d ed., trans. C. L. BEAUMONT, *The Old Testament in the Light of the Ancient East.* New York, 1911.

JEROME. *Letters and Select Works.* "A Select Library of Nicene and Post-Nicene Fathers," 2d ser., Vol. VI. New York, 1893.

———. *Liber Josue. Commentariorum in evangelium Matthaei. Opera.* Vols. IX and VII. Ed. VALLARSIUS. Verona, 1735.

———. *De situ et nominibus locorum Hebraicorum. PL,* Vol. XXIII.

JOHANNES BELETH. *Rationale divinorum officiorum. PL,* Vol. CCII.

JOHN CANTACUZENE. *Contra mohametem apologia. PG,* Vol. CLIV.

JOHN OF WÜRZBURG. *Description of the Holy Land.* Palestine Pilgrims' Text Society Edition. London, 1896.

JONAS, HANS. *The Gnostic Religion.* Boston, 1958.

JONES, H. S. V. "The Squire's Tale," in *Sources and Analogues of Chaucer's Canterbury Tales.* Ed. W. F. BRYAN and GERMAINE DEMPSTER. Chicago, 1941.

JONES, JEREMIAH. *A New and Full Method of Settling the Canonical Authority of the New Testament.* Vol. I. Oxford, 1798.

JONGE, M. DE. *The Testaments of the Twelve Patriarchs.* Assen, Netherlands, 1953.

JOSEPHUS. *Jewish Antiquities.* Ed. H. ST. J. THACKERY and RALPH MARCUS. Loeb ed. Cambridge, 1934.

JUBINAL, ACHILLE. *Mystères inédits du quinzième siècle.* Vol. II. Paris, 1837.

JULIUS AFRICANUS. *Chronography.* "Ante-Nicene Fathers," Vol. VI. Grand Rapids, Mich., 1951.

JULIUS FIRMICUS MATERNUS. *De errore profanarum religionum.* PL, Vol. XII.

JUNG, C. G. *Symbols of Transformation.* Trans. R. F. C. HULL. "Bollingen Series," Vol. XX. New York, 1956.

JUSTIN, MARTYR. *First Apology. Hortatory Address to the Greeks.* "The Ante-Nicene Fathers," Vol. I. Grand Rapids, Mich., 1956.

KABISCH, RICHARD. "Die Entstehungszeit der Apokalypse Mose," *Zeitschrift für die neutestamentliche Wissenschaft,* VI (1905), 109–34.

KAMPERS, FRANZ. *Mittelalterliche Sagen vom Paradiese und vom Holze des Kreuzes Christi.* Cologne, 1897.

KANTOROWICZ, ERNST H. *The Baptism of the Apostles.* "Dumbarton Oaks Papers," Nos. 9 and 10. Cambridge, Mass., 1956.

KATONA, LAJOS. *Magyar Tudományos Akadémia.* "Akadémiai Értesitö," XV, 97–102. Budapest, 1904.

KAUFMANN, J. "Adambuch," *Encyclopaedia Judaica,* I, 787–91. Berlin, 1928.

KAUTZSCH, E. (ed.). *Die Apokryphen und Pseudepigraphen des Alten Testaments.* Vol. II. Tübingen, 1900.

KAYSER, KARL (trans.). *Das Buch von der Erkenntniss der Wahrkeit.* Strassburg, 1893.

KER, N. R. "An Eleventh Century Old English Legend of the Cross before Christ," *Medium Aevum,* IX (1940), 84–85.

KEYSER, CHARLES E. *A List of Norman Tympana and Lintels.* London, 1904.

KINTER, WILLIAM LEWIS. "Prophetess and Fay: A Study of the Ancient and Medieval Tradition of the Sibyl." Ph. D. dissertation, Columbia University, 1958.

KOBERSTEIN, A. "Über die in Sage und Dichtung gangbare Vorstellung von dem Fortleben abgeschiedener menschlicher Seelen in der Pflanzenwelt," *Weimarisches Jahrbuch für deutsche Sprache Literatur und Kunst,* I (1854), 73–100.

KÖHLER, REINHOLD. "Zur Legende von der Königin von Saba," *Germania,* XXIX (1884), 53–58.

KOHLER, KAUFMANN. "Apple," *Jewish Encyclopedia,* II, 23–25. New York, 1902.

Bibliography 177

KOHLER, KAUFMANN. "The Essenes and the Apocalyptic Literature," *Jewish Quarterly Review*, N.S., XI (1920–21), 145–68.

KOZAK, EUGEN. "Bibliographische Übersicht der biblisch-apokryphen Literatur bei den Slaven," *Jahrbücher für protestantische Theologie*, XVIII (1892), 127–58.

KRAMER, S. N. "The Epic of Gilgameš and Its Sumerian Sources," *Journal of the American Oriental Society*, LXIV (1944), 7–23.

KUHNMUENSCH, OTTO J. *Early Christian Latin Poets from the Fourth to the Sixth Century*. Chicago, 1929.

KURFESS, ALFONS (ed. and trans.). *Sibyllinische Weissagungen*. Berlin, 1951.

LACTANTIUS. *The Epitome of the Divine Institutes*. "Ante-Nicene Christian Library," Vol. XXII. Edinburgh, 1871.

LAFORGE, EDOUARD. *La vierge, type de l'art chrétien, histoire, monuments, légendes*. Lyon, 1864.

LAGRANGE, MARIE-JOSEPH. *Le Judaïsme avant Jesus-Christ*. 3d ed. Paris, 1931.

LAJARD, FELIX. "Recherches sur le culte du cyprès pyramidal chez les peuples civilisés de l'antiquité," *Mémoires de l'institut de France. Académie des inscriptions et belles-lettres*, XX, Pt. 2 (1854), 1–292.

LAKE, KIRSOPP. "Baptism (Early Christian)," *Encyclopaedia of Religion and Ethics*, II, 379–90. New York, 1913.

LAMPE, G. W. H., and WOOLLCOMBE, K. J. *Essays on Typology*. London, 1957.

LANCHESTER, H. C. "Sibylline Oracles," *Encyclopaedia of Religion and Ethics*, XI, 496–500. New York, 1921.

LANGDON, S. "The Legend of the Kiškanu," *Journal of the Royal Asiatic Society*, 1928, pp. 843–48.

—— (ed.), *The Mythology of All Races*. Vol. V (Semitic). Boston, 1931.

LARSEN, HENNING. "Origo Crucis," in *If by Your Art. Testament to Percival Hunt*. Ed. AGNES LYNCH STARRETT. Pittsburgh, 1948.

LASCELLES, MARY M. "Alexander and the Earthly Paradise in Mediaeval English Writings," *Medium Aevum*, V (1936), 31–47, 79–104, 173–88.

LEFRANÇOIS, LOUISE PILLION. *Les sculpteurs français du XIIIe siècle*. Paris, n.d.

LIEBRECHT, FELIX. *Zur Volkskunde*. Heilbronn, 1879.

LIECHTENHAN, R. "Die pseudepigraphe Literatur der Gnostiker," *Zeitschrift für die neutestamentliche Wissenschaft*, III (1902), 222–37, 286–99.

Lipsius, Richard Adelbert. *Die apokryphen Apostelgeschichten und Apostellegenden.* Vol. I. Brunswick, 1883.

———. "Gospels Apocryphal," *A Dictionary of Christian Biography,* II, 707–9. Boston, 1880.

———. *Die Pilatus-Akten.* Kiel, 1886.

Littmann, Enno. "The Legend of the Queen of Sheba in the Tradition of Axum," *Bibliotheca Abessinica,* Vol. I. Leyden, 1904.

Longhi, Roberto. *Piero della Francesca.* 2d ed. Milan, 1942.

Loomis, C. Grant. *White Magic.* Cambridge, Mass., 1948.

Loomis, Roger Sherman. *Arthurian Tradition and Chrétien de Troyes.* New York, 1949.

Lowes, John Livingston. "The Squire's Tale and the Land of Prester John," *Washington University Studies,* I, Pt. 2, No. 1 (1913), 3–18.

Lowrie, Walter. *Art in the Early Church.* New York, 1947.

———. *Monuments of the Early Church.* New York, 1901.

Lundberg, Per. *La typologie baptismale dans l'ancienne église.* Leipzig, 1942.

Lutwin. *Adam und Eva.* Ed. Konrad Hofmann and Wilhelm Meyer. "Bibliothek des Literarischen Vereins in Stuttgart," CLIII, 1–134. Tübingen, 1881.

"Lyfe of Adam, The," "The Life of Adam and Eve," *Archiv für das Studium der neueren Sprachen und Literaturen,* LXXIV (1885), 345–65.

Mabinogion, The. Trans. Lady Charlotte Guest. Everyman ed. London, 1906.

MacCulloch, J. A. "Branches and Twigs," *Encyclopaedia of Religion and Ethics,* II, 831–33. New York, 1910.

———. *The Childhood of Fiction.* London, 1905.

———. *The Harrowing of Hell.* Edinburgh, 1930.

——— (ed.). *The Mythology of All Races.* Vol. II (Eddic). Boston, 1930.

Mackay, Cameron. "The Sign of the Palm Tree," *Church Quarterly Review,* CXXVI (1938), 187–212.

Malan, S. C. (ed. and trans.). *The Book of Adam and Eve.* London, 1882.

Mâle, Émile. *L'art religieux du XIIe siècle en France.* 3d ed. Paris, 1928.

———. *Religious Art in France in the Thirteenth Century.* Trans. from 3d ed. by Dora Nussey. London, 1913.

Malory, Sir Thomas. *The Works of Sir Thomas Malory.* Ed. Eugène Vinaver. Vol. II. Oxford, 1947.

MANDEVILLE, SIR JOHN. *Travels.* Ed. P. HAMELIUS. EETS, Vols. CLIII–CLIV. London, 1919–23.

MANLEY, JOHN MATTHEWS. "Marco Polo and the Squire's Tale," *PMLA*, XI (1896), 349–62.

MANNHARDT, WILHELM. *Germanische Mythen.* Berlin, 1858.

MARLE, RAIMOND VAN. *The Development of the Italian Schools of Painting.* Vol. III. The Hague, 1924.

MARSH, H. G. *The Origin and Significance of the New Testament Baptism.* Manchester, 1941.

MARSHALL, J. T. "Books of Adam," *A Dictionary of the Bible*, I, 37–38.

MASKELL, ALFRED. *Ivories.* London, 1905.

MAULĀNĀ MUHAMMAD 'ALI. *The Holy Qur'ān.* 4th ed. Lahore, Pakistan, 1951.

MAURY, ALFRED. *Croyances et légendes de l'antiquité.* Paris, 1863.

———. *Croyances et légendes du moyen âge.* Paris, 1896.

———. "De l'évangile de Nicodème," *Revue de philologie de littérature et d'histoire anciennes*, II (1847), 428–49.

McGIFFERT, ARTHUR CUSHMAN. *The Apostles' Creed.* New York, 1902.

MENNNER, ROBERT J. (ed.). *The Poetical Dialogues of Solomon and Saturn.* "The Modern Language Association of America Monograph Series," Vol. XIII. New York, 1941.

METZGER, BRUCE M. *An Introduction to the Apocrypha.* New York, 1957.

MEYER, WILHELM, "Die Geschichte des Kreuzholzes vor Christus," *Abhandlungen der philosophisch-philologischen Classe der Königlich Bayerischen Akademie der Wissenschaften* (Munich), XVI (1882), 103–160.

———. *Über Calderóns Sibylle des Orients.* Munich, 1879.

———. "Vita Adae et Evae," *Abhandlungen der philosophisch-philologischen Classe der Königlich Bayerischen Akademie der Wissenschaften* (Munich), XIV (1879), 187–250.

MICHAEL GLYCAS. *Annalium pars II.* PG, Vol. CLVIII.

MIGNE, JACQUES PAUL (ed. and trans.). *Dictionnaire des apocryphes.* Vol. I. Paris, 1856.

MILIK, J. T. "The Dead Sea Scrolls Fragment of the Book of Enoch," *Biblica*, XXXII (1951), 393–400.

MILLER, FRANCES H. "The Northern Passion and the Mysteries," *Modern Language Notes*, XXXXIV (1919), 88–92.

MOLAND, LOUIS. "Le drame et la légende d'Adam au moyen-âge," *Revue contemporaine*, XX (1855), 5–38.

MOLSDORF, WILHELM. *Führer durch den symbolischen und typologischen Bilderkreis der christlichen Kunst des Mittelalters.* Leipzig, 1920.

MONNIER, JEAN. *La descente aux enfers: Étude de pensée religieuse d'art et de littérature.* Paris, 1904.

MONTAULT, X. BARBIER DE. "Iconographie des sibylles," *Revue de l'art chrétien,* Vols. XIII (1869) and XIV (1870–71).

MOREY, CHARLES RUFUS. *Early Christian Art.* Princeton, 1942.

MORRIS, RICHARD (ed.). *Cursor mundi.* EETS, Vols. LVII, LIX, LXII-LXVIII-XCIX. London, 1874–78.

—— (ed.). *Legends of the Holy Rood.* EETS, Vol. XLVI. London, 1871.

MOZLEY, J. H. "Susanna and the Elders: Three Medieval Poems," *Studi medievali,* N.S., III (1930), 27–52.

——. "The *Vita Adae,*" *Journal of Theological Studies,* XXX (1929), 121–49.

MÜLLER, W. MAX (ed.). *The Mythology of All Races.* Vol. XII (Egyptian). Boston, 1918.

MUSSAFIA, ADOLPHO. "Sulla leggenda del legno della Croce," *Sitzungsberichte der philosophisch-historischen Classe der Kaiserlichen Akademie der Wissenschaften* (Vienna), LXIII (1870), 165–216.

NAPIER, ARTHUR S. (ed.). *History of the Holy Rood-Tree.* EETS, Vol. CIII. London, 1894.

NEUMAN, DOV. "Motif-Index of Talmudic-Midrashic Literature," Ph.D. dissertation, Indiana University; microfilm, Ann Arbor, Michigan, 1954.

NICOLAS, MICHEL. *Études sur les évangiles apocryphes.* Paris, 1866.

NICQUETES. *Titulus sanctae crucis.* Antwerp, 1670.

NITZE, WILLIAM A. (ed.). *Le roman de l'estoire dou graal.* Paris, 1927.

NORRIS, EDWIN (ed. and trans.). *Ancient Cornish Drama.* Vol. I. Oxford, 1854.

Notice sur Colard Mansion. Paris, 1829.

OBOLENSKY, DMITRI. *The Bogomils.* Cambridge, 1948.

ODBERG, HUGO (ed. and trans.). *3 Enoch or the Hebrew Book of Enoch.* Cambridge, 1923.

OESTERLEY, W. O. E. *The Books of the Apocrypha.* London, 1916.

——. *The Evolution of the Messianic Idea.* New York, 1908.

——. *An Introduction to the Books of the Apocrypha.* London, 1953.

OGLE, MARBURY B. "Petrus Comestor, Methodius, and the Saracens," *Speculum*, XXI (1946), 318–24.

OPPENHEIM, MAX FREIHERRN VON. *Der Tell Halaf.* Leipzig, 1931.

ORIGEN. *Commentariorum series.* "Die griechischen christlichen Schriftsteller der ersten drei Jahrhunderte," Vol. XI. Leipzig, 1933.

——. *Origen against Celsus.* "The Ante-Nicene Fathers," Vol. IV. Grand Rapids, Mich., 1956.

PARIS, PAULIN. *Les manuscrits françois de la bibliothèque du roi.* Vol. I. Paris, 1836.

——. *Les romans de la table ronde.* Vol. I. Paris, 1868.

PATAI, RAPHAEL. *Man and Temple.* London, 1947.

PATCH, HOWARD ROLLIN. *The Other World According to Descriptions in Medieval Literature.* Cambridge, Mass., 1950.

——. "Some Elements in Mediaeval Descriptions of the Otherworld," *PMLA*, XXXIII (1918), 601–43.

PAULY-WISSOWA. *Real-Encyclopädie der classischen Altertumswissenschaft*, "Oleum," Vol. XVII.

PAUPHILET, ALBERT. *Étude sur la queste del saint graal.* Paris, 1921.

——. *La queste del saint graal.* Paris, 1923.

——. "La vie terrestre d'Adam et d'Ève," *Revue de Paris*, V (1912), 213–24.

PAUSANIAS. *Description of Greece.* Trans. W. H. S. JONES. Vol. IV. Cambridge, 1935.

PEEBLES, ROSE JEFFRIES. "The Children in the Tree," in *Medieval Studies in Memory of Gertrude Schoepperle Loomis.* Paris, 1927.

——. "The Dry Tree: Symbol of Death," in *Vassar Mediaeval Studies*, ed. CHRISTABEL FORSYTHE FISKE. New Haven, 1923.

PETRUS COMESTOR. *Historia scholastica. PL*, Vol. CXCVIII.

PEUCKERT. "Dürrer Baum," in *Handwörterbuch des deutschen Aberglaubens.* Vol. II. 1930.

PFEIFFER, ROBERT. *History of New Testament Times with an Introduction to the Apocrypha.* New York, 1949.

——. "The Literature and Religion of the Pseudepigrapha," in *The Interpreter's Bible*, I, 421–36. Ed. ROBERT PFEIFFER. New York, 1952.

PFISTER, FRIEDRICH (ed. and trans.). *Der Alexanderroman des Archipresbyters Leo.* Heidelberg, 1913.

Philip, The Acts of. "Ante-Nicene Christian Library," XVI, 301–34. Edinburgh, 1870.

PINCHES, THEOPHILUS G. *The Old Testament in the Light of Historical Records and Legends of Assyria and Babylonia.* London, 1902.

PIPER, FERDINAND. "Adams Grab auf Golgatha," *Evangelisches Jahrbuch*, 1861, pp. 17–29.

——. "Der Baum des Lebens," *Evangelischer Kalender*, 1863, pp. 1–94. Trans., "The Tree of Life," *Journal of Sacred Literature*, N.S., IV (1864), 376–93; VI (1864), 27–50; VIII (1866), 57–74.

——. *Mythologie und Symbolik der christlichen Kunst.* Vol. I. Weimar, 1847.

PLATT, RUTHERFORD. *The Forgotten Books of Eden.* New York, 1927.

POTVIN, CHARLES (ed.). *Perceval le gallois ou le conte du graal.* Vol. V. Mons, 1870.

PREUSCHEN, ERWIN. "Die apokryphen gnostischen Adamschriften," *Festgruss für Bernhard Stade*, pp. 165–252. Giessen, 1900.

PRITCHARD, JAMES B. *Archaeology and the Old Testament.* Princeton, 1958.

—— (ed.). *Ancient Near Eastern Texts Relating to the Old Testament.* 2d ed. Princeton, 1955.

RABANUS MAURUS. *Commentaria in libros II Paralipomenon. PL*, Vol. CIX.

——. *De laudibus sanctae crucis. PL*, Vol. CVII.

RABY, F. J. E. *A History of Christian Latin Poetry from the Beginnings to the Close of the Middle Ages.* Oxford, 1927.

RAHNER, HUGO. *Griechische Mythen in christlicher Deutung.* Zurich, 1945.

RAMSAY, W. M. *Pauline and Other Studies.* 2d ed. New York, n.d.

RAPPOPORT, ANGELO S. *The Folklore of the Jews.* London, 1937.

——. *Mediaeval Legends of Christ.* New York, 1935.

——. *Myth and Legend of Ancient Israel.* 3 vols. London, 1928.

RAYNAUD, GASTON, and LEMAITRE, HENRI (eds.). *Le roman de Renart le contrefait.* Vol. I. Paris, 1914.

Recherches sur Louis de Bruges. Paris, 1831.

Recognitions of Clement. "The Ante-Nicene Fathers," Vol. VIII, Grand Rapids, Mich., 1951.

RENAN, ERNEST. "Fragments du livre gnostique intitulé apocalypse d'Adam ou pénitence d'Adam ou testament d'Adam," *Journal Asiatique*, LXIII (1853), 427–71.

Revelation of Moses. "Ante-Nicene Christian Library," XVI, 454–67. Edinburgh, 1870.

RIESSLER, PAUL. "Adambuch," *Lexikon für Theologie und Kirche,* I, 89–90. 1930.

———. *Altjüdisches Schriftum ausserhalb der Bibel.* Augsburg, 1928.

ROACH, WILLIAM (ed.). *The Didot Perceval According to the MSS of Modena and Paris.* Philadelphia, 1941.

RÖSCH, GUSTAV. "Die Königin von Saba als Königin Bilqîs," *Jahrbücher für protestantische Theologie* (Leipzig), VI (1880), 524–72.

ROHAULT DE FLEURY. *La Sainte Vierge.* Vol. I. Paris, 1878.

ROMAGNOLI, GAETANO (ed.). "La legienda d'Adamo e d'Eva," *Scelta di curiosità letterarie* (Bologna), CV (1870), 9–30.

ROTHSCHILD, JAMES DE. *Le mistère du viel testament.* Vol. I. Paris, 1878.

ROWLEY, H. H. *Jewish Apocalyptic and the Dead Sea Scrolls.* London, 1957.

———. *The Relevance of Apocalyptic.* 2d ed. London, 1947.

RUNCIMAN, STEVEN. *The Medieval Manichee.* Cambridge, 1947.

RYLAARSDAM, J. COERT. "Intertestamental Studies since Charles' Apocrypha and Pseudepigrapha," *The Study of the Bible Today and Tomorrow,* pp. 32–51. Ed. HAROLD R. WILLOUGHBY. Chicago, 1947.

RYLANDS, L. GORDON. *The Beginnings of Gnostic Christianity.* London, 1940.

RYLE, H. E. "Cherubim," in *A Dictionary of the Bible.* Ed. JAMES HASTINGS. Vol. I. New York, 1905.

SACKUR, ERNST. *Sibyllinische Texte und Forschungen.* Halle a.S., 1898.

SAEWULF. *The Pilgrimage of Saewulf to Jerusalem.* Palestine Pilgrims' Text Society Edition. Vol. IV. London, 1897.

SAYCE, A. H. *The Religion of the Ancient Babylonians.* 2d ed. London, 1888.

———. "The Trees of Life and Knowledge," *Florilegium Melchior de Vogüé,* pp. 543–50. Paris, 1909.

SCHLAUCH, MARGARET (ed. and trans.). *Medieval Narrative.* New York, 1928.

SCHMIDT, NATHANIEL. "The Apocalypse of Noah and the Parables of Enoch." *Oriental Studies for Paul Haupt.* Ed. CYRUS ADLER and AARON EMBER, pp. 111–23. Baltimore, 1926.

SCHOLEM, GERSHOM G. *Major Trends in Jewish Mysticism.* 2d ed. New York, 1946.

SCHRÖDER, CARL. *Van deme Holte des hilligen Cruzes.* Erlangen, 1869.

SCHÜRER, EMIL. *Geschichte des jüdischen Volkes im Zeitalter Jesu Christi.* Vol. III. 4th ed. Leipzig, 1909. Trans. (2d ed.) SOPHIE TAYLOR and PETER CHRISTIE, *A History of the Jewish People in the Time of Jesus Christ.* Edinburgh, 1886.

SCOTT, E. F. "Ophitism," *Encyclopaedia of Religion and Ethics,* IX, 499–501. New York, 1917.

SELIGSOHN, MAX. "Solomon," *The Jewish Encyclopedia,* XI, 436–48. New York, 1905.

SEYBOLT, ROBERT FRANCIS. "The *Legenda Aurea,* Bible and *Historia Scholastica,*" *Speculum,* XXI, (1946), 339–42.

SEYMOUR, WILLIAM WOOD. *The Cross in Tradition, History, and Art.* New York, 1898.

SIMPSON, CUTHBERT A. "Genesis," in *The Interpreter's Bible,* I, 439–829. New York, 1952.

SIMROCK, KARL. *Handbuch der deutschen Mythologie.* 5th ed. Bonn, 1878.

SMITH, E. BALDWIN. *Early Christian Iconography.* Princeton, 1918.

SMITH, SIDNEY. "Notes on 'The Assyrian Tree,'" *Bulletin of the School of Oriental Studies* (London), IV (1926), 69–76.

SMITH, W. ROBERTSON. *The Religion of the Semites.* New York, 1956.

SOMMER, HEINRICH OSKAR (ed.). *The Vulgate Version of the Arthurian Romances.* 7 vols. Washington, 1908–13.

SOUTHEY, ROBERT. *Omniana.* Vol. I. London, 1812.

SOZOMENUS. *The Ecclesiastical History.* "A Select Library of Nicene and Post-Nicene Fathers," 2d ser., II, 239–427. New York, 1890.

STENGEL, EDMUND (ed.). *Li romans de Durmart le galois.* Tübingen, 1873.

STONE, DARWELL. *Holy Baptism.* London, 1899.

STRAUBINGER, J. *Die Kreuzauffindungslegende.* Paderborn, 1912.

STRONG, JAMES. *The Exhaustive Concordance of the Bible.* New York, 1890.

SUCHIER, HERMANN (ed.). *Denkmäler provenzalischer Literatur und Sprache.* Vol. I. Halle, 1883.

TAYLOR, HENRY OSBORN. *The Medieval Mind.* 2 vols. 4th ed. Cambridge, Mass., 1949.

TERTULLIAN. *Against Praxeas. An Answer to the Jews. On Bap-*

tism. *Against Marcion.* "The Ante-Nicene Fathers," Vol. III. Grand Rapids, Mich., 1951.

TERTULLIAN. *Carmina adversus Marcionem. PL,* Vol. II.

THEODORUS BAR KŌNĪ. *Liber scholiorum.* "Corpus scriptorum christianorum orientalium. Scriptores Syri," Vols. XIX, XXVI. Paris, 1910, 1912.

THILO, JOHANN CARL. *Codex apocryphus novi testamenti.* Vol. I. Leipzig, 1832.

THOMPSON, R. CAMPBELL (ed.). *The Epic of Gilgamesh.* Oxford, 1930.

THOMPSON, STITH. *Motif-Index of Folk-Literature.* Rev. ed. 6 vols. Bloomington, Ind., 1955–58.

THWAITES, EDWARD (ed.). *Heptateuchus, Liber Job, et Evangelium Nicodemi, Anglo-Saxonice.* Oxford, 1698.

TISCHENDORF, CONSTANTINUS (ed.). *Apocalypses Apocryphae.* Leipzig, 1866.

—— (ed.). *Evangelia Apocrypha.* Leipzig, 1853.

TORREY, CHARLES CUTLER. *The Apocryphal Literature.* New Haven, 1945.

TRUMPP, ERNST (ed.). *Der Kampf Adams oder das christliche Adambuch des Morgenlandes.* Munich, 1880.

TWINING, LOUISA. *Symbols and Emblems of Early and Mediaeval Christian Art.* London, 1852.

VASSILIEV, A. (ed.). *Palaea historica. Anecdota graeco-byzantina,* Vol. XI, 1893.

VAUGEOIS, MARIE-EDMÉE. "Contes et légendes de Fougères," *Revue des traditions populaires,* Vol. XXI (1906).

VIAU, J. "Egyptian Mythology," in *Larousse Encyclopedia of Mythology,* pp. 8–48. New York, 1959.

VIROLLEAUD, CHARLES. "Le Roi Kéret et son fils," *Syria,* XXII (1941), 105–36, 197–217.

VOGT, FRIEDRICH. "Über Sibyllen Weissagung," *Beiträge zur Geschichte der deutschen Sprache und Literatur,* IV (1877), 48–100.

WALKER, WINIFRED. *All the Plants of the Bible.* New York, 1957.

WARNER, RUBIE D.-N. (ed.). *Early English Homilies from the Twelfth Century. MS Vesp. D XIV.* EETS, Vol. CLII. London, 1917.

WARREN, C. "Golgotha," "Hebron," "Machpelah," *A Dictionary of the Bible.* Ed. JAMES HASTINGS. Vols. II and III. New York, 1903, 1906.

WARREN, F. E. *The Liturgy and Ritual of the Ante-Nicene Church.* London, 1897.

WATSON, ARTHUR. *The Early Iconography of the Tree of Jesse.* London, 1934.

WATTS, ALAN W. *Myth and Ritual in Christianity.* London, 1953.

WEIL, GUSTAV. *Biblische Legenden der Müselmänner.* Frankfurt, 1845. Trans. *The Bible, the Koran and the Talmud.* New York, 1863.

WESSELOFSKY, ALEXANDER. "Altslavische Kreuz- und Rebensagen," *Russische Revue,* XIII (1878), 130–52.

WESTON, JESSIE L. "The Apple Mystery in Arthurian Romance," *Bulletin of the John Rylands Library,* IX (1925), 417–30.

WHITTREDGE, RUTH (ed.). *La nativité et le geu des trois roys.* Bryn Mawr, Pa., 1944.

WIDENGREN, GEO. "The Ascension of the Apostle and the Heavenly Book"; "The King and the Tree of Life in Ancient Near Eastern Religion"; "Mesopotamian Elements in Manichaeism," *Uppsala Universitets Årsskrift,* 1950:7; 1951:4; 1946:3.

WILLARD, RUDOLF. *Two Apocrypha in Old English Homilies.* "Beiträge zur englischen Philologie," Vol. XXX. Leipzig, 1935.

WILSON, R. McL. *The Gnostic Problem.* London, 1958.

WÜLCKER, RICHARD PAUL. *Das Evangelium Nicodemi in der abendländischen Literatur.* Marburg, 1872.

WÜNSCHE, AUGUST. *Die Sagen vom Lebensbaum und Lebenswasser.* Ex Oriente Lux, I, 2/3. Leipzig, 1905.

YULE, SIR HENRY (trans. and ed.). *The Book of Ser Marco Polo.* Vol. I, rev. HENRI CORDIER. 3d ed. London, 1903.

—— (ed.). *The Travels of Odoric of Pordenone in Cathay and the Way Thither.* Vol. II. 2d ed. Hakluyt Society, 2d ser., Vol. XXXIII. London, 1913.

ZARNCKE, FRIEDRICH. "Der Priester Johannes." *Abhandlungen der philologisch-historischen Classe der Königlich sächsischen Gesellschaft der Wissenschaften* (Leipzig), VII (1879), 827–1030; VIII (1883), 1–186.

ZEITLIN, SOLOMON. "Jewish Apocryphal Literature," *Jewish Quarterly Review,* N.S., XL (1949–50), 223–50.

ZÖCKLER, OTTO. *Die Apokryphen des Alten Testament.* Munich, 1891.

——. *Das Kreuz Christi.* Gütersloh, 1875. Trans. MAURICE J. EVANS, *The Cross of Christ,* London, 1877.

ZOTENBERG, M. HERMANN (ed. and trans.). *Chronique de Tabari.* Paris, 1867.

ZUNZ, LEOPOLD. *Die gottesdienstlichen Vorträge der Juden.* Frankfurt a.M., 1892.

INDEX

The Quest of Seth

Index   191

Haggada, 16
Harlot, 12; prophesies, 9, 51, 52, 59; sits on tree, 51, 52, 55, 56, 57, 59; as "Sibilla," 52, 60; as "Susanna," 52, 62
Hat-hôr, 121
Healing(s), 24, 26, 27, 63, 65, 84; serpent as symbol of, 115
Heaven, 22, 93, 106; tree reaches Heaven, 117, 125
Hebrew; see Jewish
Hebron, 2, 73, 74, 75, 76, 106
Helena, Saint, 3, 52, 57; discovery of the cross, 49, 57
Hell: Christ's descent into, 35, 37, 41, 44, 45; roots of tree extend into, 106, 117, 125
Herb of immortality, 94
Herbs, 32, 96
Hermes, 91
Hermes Criophore, 122
Herodotus, 72
Hiontus, 10, 71; see also Jonitus
Historia, 10, 11, 62–66, 69, 70, 72, 73
Historia de Preliis, 112
Holy Spirit, 51, 106; represented by pine, 51, 52, 58, 106
Honorius of Autun, 10, 69, 72, 73, 76; see also *De imagine mundi*

Immortality, 18, 20, 21, 22, 23, 24, 77, 78, 91, 94, 98, 115; see also Eternal life
Irenaeus, 74
Isaiah, 25, 58, 77

Jacobus de Voragine, 104, 129, 130
James, Montague Rhodes, 30
Jerome, 75, 76
Jerusalem, 51, 52, 66, 73, 74, 82, 106, 128, 130
Jesse, 77, 78, 120; see also Tree of Jesse
Jesus, 107, 129; as child in tree, 117, 120, 125, 126
Jew(s), 3, 23, 28, 51, 63, 107, 129; Alexandrian, 15, 27, 60
Jewish: origin of Seth legend, 8; apocalyptic literature, 17; apocrypha, 19, 20, 21, 26, 30, 77, 95; legend(s), 26, 71, 74, 92, 93, 101; tradition, 74, 75, 94

Johannes Beleth, 11, 12, 81, 88, 99, 129, 130
John, 66
John (the Apostle), 111, 112
John the Baptist, 39, 41
Jonitus, 70, 71; see also Hiontus
Jordan, 39, 40, 41, 45, 88, 89, 90, 97, 99, 100
Josephus, 72
Journey: of Seth, 8, 9, 15, 16, 21, 28, 32, 39, 46, 88, 91, 92, 94, 96, 99; to Paradise, 17, 21, 23, 24, 30, 91, 108; of Gilgamesh, 21; to the other world, 22, 38; of Enoch, 23, 24, 29, 71
Judas, 51, 52, 55
Julius Africanus, 75
Jung, C. G., 94, 126

Keret, 17, 20; legend, 18, 20, 24, 30
Keret, Epic of, 17
Kernel(s), 2, 12; of tree of knowledge, 10, 72, 73, 74, 76, 77, 83, 84; see also Seed(s)
King, dying, 19, 20; see also Father
III Kings, 64, 65
Kohler, K., 28
Koran, 79, 80, 83

Leaves, 26, 27; tree with three kinds of, 63; twig with three, 88, 90, 98, 100
Lebanon, 58
Legenda Aurea, 129; Caxton's translation of, 4
Legende, 11, 12, 53, 55, 103–30, 134
Leo, Archpriest, 112
Liber Floridus, 111
Llew Llaw Gyffes, 109
Loomis, Roger Sherman, 7, 118

MacCulloch, J. A., 42
Malak-Bêl, 122
Malory, Sir Thomas, *Morte Darthur*, 5
Mandeville, Sir John, *Travels*, 4, 113
Marah, 2, 53
Marco Polo, 113
Martyr, 62, 107, 129

192

Index   193

Seth); of son, 20; of St. Helena, 57; of Gilgamesh, 91

Ra, 121
Rabbinic literature, 23, 26
Ram, 122, 123
Raphael, 76
Rappoport, A. S., 6, 29
Rationale divinorum officiorum, 11, 88, 99, 129
Rebirth: baby in tree as symbol, 12, 105, 125, 127; seeds as symbol, 12, 105
Recognitions of Clement, 26
Redemption, 8, 10, 12, 41, 45, 49, 74, 98, 136; *see also* Salvation
Reine pédauque, 78
Resurrection, 35, 74, 75, 112, 121
Rod: of Moses, 50, 55, 58, 71, 93; of Jesse, 120
Rods: of Moses, 9, 51, 52, 57, 58; of David, 51, 52, 57, 59; become one tree, 52; cannot be moved, 52
Rood-tree legend(s), 6, 9, 10, 49–66, 69–84, 87; in Slavonic, 6, 53, 54, 55, 56, 57, 58, 61, 71, 96, 98, 101; merged with Seth legend, 11, 32, 87–101, 103–30; *see also* Cross; Wood

Sackur, Ernst, 70
Salvation, 51, 74, 76, 77, 98, 107; *see also* Redemption
Satanael, 53, 56
Savior, 75, 100, 125; *see also* Christ
Seed(s), 105, 127, 128; from Paradise, 10; three, 106, 107, 127; *see also* Kernel(s)
Serpent, 21; in the tree, 2, 12, 106, 114–17, 128; *see also* Adder; Snake
Seth (Egyptian sun deity), 29
Seth (son of Adam), 2, 8, 9, 11, 12, 16, 22, 23, 27, 28–30, 42, 43, 46, 56, 91, 92, 98, 104, 107, 115, 118; type of Christ, 4; gets herbs, 32, 95, 96; gets twig, 71, 88, 90, 93, 94, 95, 96, 97, 99, 100, 101; goes to Paradise, 88, 99, 105, 109; plants twig on Adam's grave, 89, 90, 99; sees baby in tree, 106, 117,

124; sees dry tree, 106, 110; sees serpent in tree, 106, 114; gets three seeds, 109, 127
Seth legend, 15–32; combined with rood-tree legend, 2–9, 11–12, 87–101, 103–30; in drama, 4, 5, 6; in English literature, 4, 5; in art, 5; Jewish origin, 8; in Greek, 8, 15–31; in Latin, 8, 31–32; Christian adoption, 9, 32, 35–46; *see also* Journey; Quest
Sethites, 29
Sha'taqat, 17
Sheba, Queen of, 10, 11, 82, 130; refuses to walk on bridge, 11, 81, 100, 130; refuses to sit on tree, 55; merged with sibyl, 61, 73; visits Solomon, 61, 65, 73, 78, 81, 84; prophesies, 74, 78, 82, 83, 84, 89; as Bilkis, 80; *see also* Queen of South
Shem, 76
Sibilla, 52, 57, 60, 61, 62
Sibyl, 3, 60; as prophetess, 60, 65, 130; merged with Queen of Sheba, 61, 64, 65, 72, 73, 78; as harlot, 62
Sibylla, Queen of the South, 107
Sibylline Oracles: sixth book, 60; eighth or acrostic book, 83, 130
Siloe, 107, 129
Silver, 64; hoop(s) around tree, 51, 52, 55; rings around tree, 55, 128
Simrock, Karl, 78
Sin, 2, 12, 20, 44, 76, 77, 105, 106, 108, 109, 110, 111, 112, 114; of Adam, 74
Sivila, Queen, 53
Smyrna; *see* Myrrha
Snake, 105; in tree, 108; *see also* Adder; Serpent
Solomon, 2, 9, 10, 11, 51, 53, 58, 59, 60, 61, 63, 64, 65, 66, 70, 72, 73, 74, 78, 79, 80, 81, 82, 83, 84, 100, 107, 128, 129; his small half brother, 73, 83
Son (of God), 51; represented by cedar, 51, 52, 58; represented by cypress, 106

Date Due

APR 2 5 1984		
10-21-91 PAB		
IL # 4096325		
DUE 11-21-91		
IL: 4407025		
SRU: 5-24-93		
Due: 6-20-93		

Demco 293-5